Dear Ann

I hope this book

inspires and helps you

find your passion

Best of luck

David

POSITIVEROSITY

'David has an infectious sense of adventure, a selfless community spirit and a fire in the belly that gives everyone around him the belief in their dreams. I've purposefully spent as much time as possible with David over the past decade, because in a world of doubters and set-backs, he shares my desire to step out and do things differently.'
MARK BEAUMONT
ROUND THE WORLD IN 80 DAYS
RECORD-BREAKING CYCLIST

'There are not many people who can make a 54 mile hike in 24 hours a really fun event but David is one of them. Just when you've had enough, in the middle of nowhere, there's a fire-breathing dragon, an ice cream stall, a serving of haggis, fireworks over a remote loch... and so it goes on.'
POLLY MURRAY
ADVENTURER AND FIRST SCOTTISH
WOMAN TO CLIMB EVEREST

'This book should be compulsory reading for everyone. It is packed with inspiring and uplifting life lessons for success. David has discovered that the difference between 'ordinary' and 'extraordinary' simply requires commitment to our vision, our motivation and most importantly our action taking. I cannot recommend this book highly enough.'
ROBIN SIEGER
AUTHOR OF INTERNATIONAL BEST-
SELLER *NATURAL BORN WINNERS,*
AND PEAK PERFORMANCE EXPERT

'David Fox-Pitt is A great man who continues to do so much to encourage adventure in young people in the UK!'
BEAR GRYLLS
CHIEF SCOUT

'My cousin David is the most extraordinary force. His positivity runs through every vein in his body. His energy combined with his brilliant unique imagination has led him to create fantastic events that provide challenges and fun for the participants but also raise millions for good causes.'
WILLIAM FOX-PITT
OLYMPIC MEDALIST AND
INTERNATIONALLY ACCLAIMED
THREE DAY EVENTER

'David is a bundle of positive energy whose main aim in life seems to be concocting ever more challenging ways for people to suffer, and in doing so, inspire themselves out of their comfort zone, and along the road to personal improvement and self belief.'
ROB WAINWRIGHT
FORMER CAPTAIN OF THE
SCOTTISH RUGBY TEAM

'If only positivity could be purchased. David's book is a great alternative. His can-do attitude is infectious and inspirational.'
NEIL LAUGHTON
EXPLORER & ADVENTURER

First published January 2018
by Maida Vale Publishing Ltd
Suite 333, 19-21 Crawford Street
London, W1H 1PJ
United Kingdom

Cover design by Sacha Fox-Pitt
Graphic design by Edwin Smet
Cover photograph by Malcolm Cochrane Photography
Printed in England by TJ International Ltd, Padstow, Cornwall

The moral right of David Fox-Pitt to be identified as
author of this work has been asserted in accordance with section 77
of the Copyright, Designs and Patents Act 1988

Eyewear wishes to thank James Gilbertson of ASANOX
for introducing David's great work to us.

Set in Bembo 12,8 / 17 pt
ISBN 978-1-908998-51-4

WWW.EYEWEARPUBLISHING.COM

DAVID FOX-PITT

Positiverosity 7 Golden Principles

∞ MAIDA VALE PUBLISHING

An imprint of Eyewear Publishing

DEDICATION

I would like to dedicate this book to my family. My father, Mervyn, always an inspiration in positiverosity, has been a massive influence in my life. My mother, Janet, taught me the importance of generosity by her example of overwhelming kindness to all she meets. My two sisters Miranda and Leonie, both talented artists who support me in so many ways and my wife, Joanna who has helped write this book. Her constant belief in me and abundant patience enables me to follow my dreams so that together we can support our three children as they discover their own purpose and passions.

TABLE OF CONTENTS

INTRODUCTION
—
THE WILD FOX WAY

On the 2nd of July, 2015, I cycled 100 miles on a penny-farthing. Yes, that kind of penny-farthing. The one invented in the 1870s, that Victorians used to ride around on. The one with the enormous front wheel and tiny back one, that you have to climb onto when the thing is moving, then attempt to balance on top of, one and a half metres in the air. Not only did I take on this monumental 100-mile challenge, but I persuaded my great friend and fellow Scot, Mark Beaumont, to join me on another of these contraptions.

At that time Mark was already an international long-distance cycling legend and had just returned from his African trip from Cairo to Cape Town, a total distance of ten thousand kilometres, which he had completed in forty-two days and eight hours. One hundred miles on a penny-farthing? No problem. Me? Well, I'd done a quick training circuit around Loch Tay – that should suffice.

Where did I get the idea to do this ride? My company WildFox Events was about to launch the Etape Royale, a 100-mile closed road cycle sportive that starts and finishes in Ballater, Aberdeenshire. The route takes you through Moray, the Lecht and along the banks of the River Dee, encompassing a challenging mix of rolling scenery, tough climbs and alpine-esque descents among a wild and empty landscape. With 9829 feet of total ascent, armchair onlookers commented that the route, while spectacular, was perhaps a bit over the heads of the likely participants, who were mostly fair-weather weekend cyclists wishing to lose a few pounds from their central belts. What we needed was a challenge to test the event's viability, and prove to the naysayers that it could be done.

What better opportunity for me to take my penny-farthing out for a spin? Compared to some of the challenges I've faced, many of which you'll read about later on in this book, 100 miles of cycling sounded like a piece of cake – on a normal bike, that is. Penny-farthings don't have gears. Their fixed wheel design predates the idea of gears or suspension, with the purpose of the oversized front wheel being to generate more speed with less pedalling. On the other hand, the disadvantage of the large, slim wheel is that it is very unstable, and riding the bike becomes extremely dangerous. With no suspension, even the slightest bump in the road or the gentlest of descents can catapult you rapidly from a seated position 56 inches in the air to flat on the hard road in an instant. It's like falling off a horse – and I should know. I grew up around horses – William Fox-Pitt of three-day eventing and Olympic fame being my first cousin.

After a bit of practice and showing Mark how to correctly mount the penny-farthing – a miracle of balance and co-ordination in and of itself – we were on our way. 'High ho silver.' At first, everything seemed to be going well. The road was smooth, the scenery absolutely breathtaking, the company stimulating. When we reached the first big ascent, though, the drawbacks of the penny-farthing became clearer. One gear is simply not enough to climb Scotland's hills, and, for the first time since we were children, Mark and I found ourselves dismounting and wheeling our bikes up some of the steeper ascents as we looked forward to the next downhill section, taking our feet off the pedals and letting that giant wheel do its job as we raced down. What freedom! Race down we did, at speeds greater than anticipated. With braking being such an inexact science on a penny-farthing, we were in very real danger of falling off and seriously injuring ourselves. Victorian newspapers are full of stories of unfortunate enthusiasts taking a 'header' and suffering severe and often fatal injuries. I knew of the dangers, but I wasn't scared. As a reserve in the paras and SAS I was confident that I could get myself out of any situation, but, at mile eighty, whilst descending a 20% gradient from the Lecht Ski Centre I lost control at breakneck speed, and despite wrestling to regain control of the bike, I found myself flying through the air with the penny-farthing spinning above me. Hitting the deck, I was convinced I'd suffered serious injury. Shock and severe pain were what I felt most at first, and when I reached to remove my helmet, I saw that it had split completely in half. Mark was able to dismount before making the same mistake, having witnessed my over-zealous stunt. To think that helmet could have been my skull gave me the shivers. Still, with only twenty miles to go, I couldn't give up yet. With Mark's encouragement, I brushed myself down, miraculously finding no broken bones. I straightened up the handlebars, re-aligned the back wheel and climbed back on my bike, and together we completed the challenge.

Typically, an average cyclist can finish a 100-mile ride (or a century, as the feat is known to cyclists) in five hours or so. Completing the course on a penny-farthing, with its lack of gears, took 13 hours and 40 minutes. I was completely exhausted. The ride had been much harder than I had thought it would be, and Mark, even after all his adventures, later commented that the 100 miles on a penny-farthing was one of the most painful things he has ever done. Perhaps he was simply trying to make me feel better.

I first met Mark when he was looking for a sponsor for his first round the world trip. He was put in touch with me by my adventurer friend Neil Laughton, and Mark came up to meet me at my home on the shores of Loch Tay. After chatting with him for a few minutes in our kitchen, it soon became clear that this young man in his mid-twenties was not only determined, but had what it takes – Can Do. He had a plan and nothing was going to stop him. Mark was on a mission coupled with a powerful sense of self-belief. Let's bottle this magic for a moment, and dissect what happened over the kitchen table. What was it that caught my attention? He had resolve, faith in his abilities, and the passion to pull off his plan. The very next day I was in Edinburgh with him and introduced him to Artemis (loyal sponsors of WildFox Events). Artemis fund managers have been his primary sponsor ever since.

On the 18th September 2017 Mark broke the boundaries of possible by completing his journey in an astonishing 79 days, smashing the round the world cycling record by 44 days and beating his own previous record – set in 2008 – by 115 days. Like his first circumnavigation in 2008, I was there to meet him in Paris, only this time I joined him for the final furlong to the Arc de Triomphe on my penny-farthing. Dressed in my Delmonte white linen jacket and pith helmet along with Neil Laughton, on another penny-farthing in his long tail coat and top hat, and my wife Jo, on a traditional ladies' bike, we were no doubt an eccentric sight – but Phileas Fogg would have approved. Mark, you are such an inspiration, and how proud we were to share that moment with you. He arrived and was greeted by a representative of the Guinness Book of Records amid the snarling jumble of Paris rush hour traffic and a mass of photographers, press, well-wishers, family and friends. What a hero. Can you imagine what it takes to cycle over 240 miles a day for over two and a half months?

The penny-farthing was the first machine to be called a bicycle and the story of how this machine has evolved over the intervening 150 years graphically illustrates what can be achieved through positive human endeavour, invention, innovation and raw determination. The penny-farthing was the beginnings of cycling as a sport, and spawned a new urge for athleticism and endurance challenges as a part of everyday life.

Our trip on those cranky dinosaurs in the Aberdeenshire hills was an achievement in itself given our mode of transport, but the journey that led Mark to his triumphant arrival in Paris was totally off-the-scale miraculous. What can we learn from Mark? How can we develop the skills he demonstrates in abundance? How can we infuse others with this power of self-belief? What does it take to acquire these qualities (or is one simply born that way?) and how can such attributes also be transferred to our everyday lives, in business, management and logistical planning?

It has been a privilege to be a small part of Mark's amazing journey. He continues to inspire thousands to take that leap of faith as we follow his infectious drive. He absolutely underscores the principles I have set out in this book.

That penny-farthing trip with Mark was testing – it was designed to be so. I've always liked to test myself and my friends to keep us on our toes – but I've had plenty of other more dramatic escapades. In my time I've climbed the Carstensz Pyramid, hitch-hiked from Paris to Athens, ran 173 kilometres in 45 hours, passed SAS selection, been trapped on a volcano in New Zealand for three days, and had many, many more adventures – some wonderful, some difficult, but all memorable. I love being outside and being active and would have done them all purely for the thrill of it; however, I've more than often made it all the more rewarding by injecting a fundraising element into what I do. I would have expected all of these experiences to be eye-opening in some way, but never could have imagined the magnitude of the lessons they have taught me, and the ways in which each one has shaped my life. In this book, I will tell you some of my tales, and explain the impact each of them had on me, in the hope of enlightening you in the same way, so that you can take what I have learned even further, and gain the vital skills you need to set off on the adventure of your own life.

So, going back to the penny-farthing trip with Mark, why again did I cycle 100 miles on a penny-farthing? Why suffer willingly, when we could have easily avoided the extreme discomfort? Is it all about the challenge? Yes and no. I admit I like a challenge, as I'm sure you've already gathered, but I like doing it for a purpose. The purpose this time was not only to promote my new event, the Etape Royale, and to fundraise for earthquake victims in Nepal, but as founder of WildFox Events, the company I set up to raise money for charitable causes all over the world through adventure charities, I've always felt like I shouldn't encourage people to do something that I wouldn't do myself – with bells on. The story of my company WildFox Events cannot be told without the stories of my adventures: for me, they go hand in hand. Everything is connected.

WildFox adventure challenges are visceral. The momentum of mass participation spurs each individual who takes part in an event to find reserves of gritty determination and physical stamina they didn't know they had. As the events take place outdoors, among some of the most remote and extraordinary areas of the world, the elements can be extreme, and there is always a sense of urgency, as well as fun. On a WildFox event, you must expect the unexpected. I take great pleasure in adding in surprises with an eccentric twist to cheer on the participants – I once put an Elvis impersonator and a fire-breathing dragon in the woods to entertain walkers in the middle of a long hike! I like to set up impromptu water stops to raise spirits when the going gets tough. 'Keep at it!' I cheer, 'you're nearly there!' I love creating opportunities for people to learn more about themselves through testing themselves to their very limits – I have found on my journey that this is where our true nature becomes evident to us, and where we can access what we are truly capable of. A WildFox Event will give you the certainty that you are able to achieve whatever you set your mind to. I set up the company with nothing but a dream, and its huge impact is a testament to the lessons I learned along the way. I hope that by sharing these fundamental nuggets of wisdom I can in some way inspire and encourage 'can do' in others.

To date, WildFox has raised over £40 million to support charities all around the world, through sponsorship, donation and participation in the events. Both national and international charities have felt the benefits of my work, and I also take pride in boosting local economies by bringing thousands of people to enjoy the particular natural beauty and charm of an area. The Etape Royale, for example, did wonders for the community of Ballater. Only months before the event, it had been hit first by fire, when its historic railway station burned down, then by cataclysmic flooding. Many homes and businesses were left six feet underwater, and the influx of visitors, both participants of the event, and the friends and family who accompanied them to cheer them on and greet them in droves as they crossed the finish line, helped

the town enormously in getting back on its feet.

Of course, I would never ask any participant to set off on an adventure that I had not completed myself. I have weathered them all in the most extreme of circumstances, not least the Glencoe Marathon Gathering during a harsh January blizzard. Possibly the hardest, though, was the Artemis Great Kindrochit Quadrathlon. The Quad is arguably Scotland's toughest one-day event. The course goes like this: a 0.8 mile swim across Loch Tay, a run over seven Munros (these are mountains in Scotland with heights of 3000 feet) including Ben Lawers, a seven-mile kayak and finally a 34-mile cycle ride around the perimeter of Loch Tay. Since it began, it has raised over nine million pounds, mainly for Mercy Corps, and more recently for Mary's Meals.

I first planned the route as I sat at my home, Kindrochit, on the banks of Loch Tay, one balmy spring morning eighteen years ago. The task seemed enormous – I wasn't sure if it was even possible. Could the human body endure such a mammoth endeavour? In the October of that year, I set out with three friends to attempt it. It was more Wacky Races than professional elite event – today's strict kit checks and risk assessments would certainly not have passed a bin liner as a waterproof coat, or footwear that could best be described as bedroom slippers. We were ill-prepared, and narrowly avoided disaster when one team member started showing symptoms of hypothermia during the kayak phase. We decided we had rather give up the attempt than risk losing one of our crew, so we abandoned the expedition and set off home with heavy hearts. Had I had been too ambitious after all? Maybe the task really was impossible. However, the idea still burned within me, only growing stronger each time I looked out of my window over the loch. I found I simply could not give the idea up. My eternal optimism and indomitable spirit told me I could and would finish the course I had laid out in my mind, and eventually, I succeeded. I knew then that I could make a go of it, and with sponsorship from Artemis Investment Management, the event grew from strength to strength and has changed the lives of many thousands of people.

The Quad is perhaps our most difficult event, but WildFox has created and is associated with many other events over the last twenty years. The Caledonian Challenge, a 54-mile hike through the West Highland Way in just 24 hours, has raised close to £13 million for Scottish communities via the Scottish Community Foundation. Maggie's Monster Bike and Hire has seen 8000 participants cycle 31 miles, followed by a 9, 23 or 41-mile hike along the stunning Great Glen Way to raise £6 million for Maggie's, a charity that supports cancer sufferers and their families. The Rob Roy Challenge consists of a walk and cycle over 56 miles from Drymen to Kenmore, and has raised over £4 million for Habitat for Humanity, Site Savers International, Water Aid, the Prince's Trust, Cancer Research UK and Barnardo's among others since it started in 2006. These are just a few – WildFox events also launched the Artemis Highland 100 (a 100km cycle challenge in Perthshire), the Pentland Push (a 26.2 mile hike with 2047 metres of hills to climb), the Loch Ness Marathon, the Bank of Scotland Corporate Cairngorm Mountain Bike Challenge, the Oxfam Tailtrekker, the Cateran Yomp, the Loch Lomond Challenge, the Hearts and Heroes Challenge, the Hannibal Challenge, the D-Day 44 Challenge on the Normandy beaches and the Three Peaks Challenge. The expertise I learned from organising these events also helped me found my own charity, Project Northern Lights, which works to improve the lives and prospects for young people in Scotland though workshops teaching skills from basic joinery and metalwork to using advanced laser cutting technology. WildFox have also partnered with other organisations such as British Schools Exploring Society, Next Generation and Score Against the Law, all focussed on creating opportunities for young people.

Why work so hard to make so much money, just to give it all away? The answer is simple – I believe that the effect WildFox can have on lives all over the world is worth all the pain and effort I put myself through on these challenges. If I can inspire and motivate even hundreds of people to make a difference, then I will have changed the world in my own way. Knowing that my short-term suffering will change other people's lives unimaginably for the better makes me push myself all the harder – can you imagine any motivation more powerful and rewarding? Compassion is the key, and I believe the world needs a whole lot more of this medicine. Our mantra is to encourage everyone to think of a way that they can make a difference in other peoples' lives, and the Wild Fox way is a way of bettering yourself through philanthropy, and of exercising your passion, perseverance, positiverosity, planning, purpose, patience, and practicality. I believe

these seven skills are essential for success, and lie at the heart of every great mission. In this book, I will talk you through each of them, sharing the stories of how I came to discover them, as well as my advice for using them to make your life into your own adventure. I hope that you will be inspired to use this book to leave your own unique mark on the world, with or without a penny-farthing!

POINTS FOR REFLECTION

- Our thoughts become objective things.

- Every thought we hold in our consciousness for any length of time becomes impressed upon our sub-conscious mind, and creates a pattern which the mind weaves into our life and environment – so let's make our thoughts wholesome and positive.

- Honesty is the first chapter of the book of wisdom.

- Do not depend upon your memory alone, to do so will destroy your power of thought and it is thought that leads to wisdom.

- The germ of defeat is in every selfish thought.

- A truly great man or woman never puts away the simplicity of a child.

CHAPTER 1
PURPOSE – THE SEVEN-DAY HITCHIKE TO ATHENS

Purpose: a lesson in humility, understanding, and what really drives people in life.

Let's start at the beginning: the first step on the path to success and fulfilment. In this chapter, I'm going to tell you about purpose, and show you how I came to discover its unique power when I got stranded in Paris on my way to Athens.

It was 1982, I was eighteen years old, and I'd just made plans to meet up with a friend – in a small seaside village near the Corinth Canal in Greece. I had always had a vague dream of one day travelling through Europe, and now was the time; the legendary Magic Bus travelled from Paris to Athens, I had the name of the village in Greece – that was good enough. Adventure was the name of the game: I didn't bother with an address or telephone number, and arrived in Paris with the intention of following the transcontinental hippie trail, only to find out that the Magic Bus was fully booked. I'd like to hold it right there for one moment and explain a vital rule I live my life by. It is 'be bold and never falter from your purpose'. I didn't know it then, but it's well-explained by the Theory of Goethendipity of Johann Wolfgang von Goethe (1749-1832): 'Until one is committed there is hesitancy. A chance to draw back. Always ineffectiveness concerning all acts of initiative and creation. There is one elementary proof, the ignorance of which kills countless ideas and splendid plans. This is, that the moment one definitely commits oneself then providence moves too. All sorts of things occur to help one, that would never otherwise have occurred. A whole stream of events issues from the decision, raising in one's favour all manor of unforeseen incidents and material assistance, which no man could have dreamed would have come his way. Whatever you can do or dream you can begin it! Boldness has genius, power and magic in it, begin it now.'

Begin it now. Well, my defiant teenage mind said 'bugger it'. I had started the journey and there was no way I was giving up now. I held on to my purpose and carried on. So began the ambitious Seven Day Hitchhike To Athens, fuelled by youthful audacity and poorly-thought out decisions. Did I have enough cash? What happened if I ran out, or if no one stopped to pick me up? Would it help if I wore a kilt to signal that I was not a threat, or played the bagpipes?... I did not have my kilt, and I could not play the pipes.

I was lucky in that my first day's thumbing took me straight to the South of France from Paris. Hey, this hitchhiking game wasn't so bad! Feeling smug on my first drop-off, late at night near Aix-en-Provence, I set up camp and crashed out for the night.

I managed to continue hitching along the south coast of France, arriving on the Nice seafront in the early evening of Day Two. After wolfing down a baguette au fromage, I was so tired I just rolled out my straw mat (the modern inflatable ones had not been invented then) and lay down on the beach. Hitchhiking is no mere pastime. It's mentally and physically exhausting: hours standing in a lonely lay-by thumbing for lifts, being humiliated as car after car rushes past without recognising you as a human. As an ordinary, self-centred teenager it was a sharp lesson that the world would not naturally accommodate itself to my desires. But this did not trouble me at first. There were other sleepers on the beach that night and the gentle rhythm of the waves soon sent me into a deep sleep, with visions of Corinthian beaches and bronzed bikinied beauties dancing in my head.

I was under cool water, surfacing at the foot of a waterfall. Water was pouring onto my face... I could feel the force of it driving onto my head... when suddenly I was hit directly by a jet of water so powerful that I leapt off my mat and fell face-first into a pile of sand. 'Help! Bastards!' I shouted incoherently, still half-asleep. My innocent righteousness was misplaced: the Nice Municipal Police were hosing all the campers down, as it was illegal to sleep on the beach. However indignant I felt, I had to set off along the shore. It must have been 4am as I grabbed my belongings and stuffed them into the rucksack, still in a daze. Here, I was not my mother's son: I was a bum like any other – and I had to realise that there was no reason why the police would treat me differently.

Hitchhiking for only two days and I'd already learned to see myself as others saw me. What are they thinking? was the question that obsessed me – and I couldn't be squeamish about it. In all my life, I'd never spent more time considering how I looked, and this was ironic, as I was scruffy, unshaven, and certainly not at my best.

I was also learning patience. It could be hours sometimes before a car would stop, and the driver could be travelling for just a few miles, so that I'd have to swallow back my frustration when thanking them, before starting the process of begging all over again. I quickly realised how spoilt it was to expect that others would feel kind enough to pick me up or ask where I wanted to go – and how extraordinary those were who did. My purpose – to reach Greece – was one that did not involve or interest anyone else, and I began to understand the natural human tendency to expect things to happen quickly, and to get annoyed if aims don't work out as intended. It was humiliating to feel so powerless in pursuit of my goal, but all I could do was stand and hope.

Hitching along the south coast of France in those first few days, I clearly remember watching some birds as I was standing in a rainstorm, feeling pretty glum and self-pitying. The birds, taking shelter in the branches of a tree, were still twittering – just waiting out the bad weather, adjusting their pattern of life and carrying on. Adapting and adjusting to what we can't control is an important part of growing up and hitchhiking teaches patience, resilience, and gives an important perspective on human nature and behaviour.

I reached Monaco, then San Remo and then I was stuck. It was literally impossible to get a lift. I soon discovered that Italians are not in the habit of picking up strangers, and eventually, after five solid hours of waiting, my thumb was exhausted, and I decided I had no choice but to take the train from Genoa to Trieste. This made a major dent in my financial planning, giving me very little to travel through Yugoslavia, Macedonia and then Greece. Hitchhiking normally goes hand in hand with being penniless, and obviously aged eighteen I had limited funds. Well, as well as lessons in the moral virtue of humility, at least I was also getting a practical lesson in conserving funds and prioritising how I spent my money.

Having blown most of my budget on the

train, and despite missing a few breakfasts and keeping an eye out for coins in gutters, I finally ran out of cash halfway down Yugoslavia. I only got through by relying on handouts from a couple of very kind German drivers who gave me lifts and food. I was learning how desperate life without money is. For the first time I really saw the beggars on the streets around me (a constant presence in Europe's towns and cities then, as today). They were people just like me – I too was experiencing, on a smaller scale, the depravations that plague so many of our fellow human beings, and was beginning to feel true compassion for those people who have nothing. It is one of the experiences I am most grateful for: rather than my original pity or queasy feeling of guilt, suffering hunger and deprivation myself meant that inside me a desire was building up to actually do something about it. With an energetic, eighteen-year-old sense of injustice, I asked myself: how many people have to go through this every day, week and month of their lives; begging, scraping, selling their bodies in order to eat? How can we create a society where all can eat at least one decent meal a day?

Putting yourself in someone else's shoes gives you perspective on your own limited point of view. Basically, all it took was for me to leave my normal, comfortable life in a First World country and experience hunger – and it was a lesson worth learning. In my mind, there should be more value placed on humility and empathy in society. It would be interesting to see if this could be taught through a practical regime. Imagine a 'Humility Programme', where participants spent a week sleeping rough and also going low on food for several days! OK, that sounds a little like some kind of sci-fi punishment (or a typical Western gap year). I'm only half joking. When we have so much in this world, it is disgraceful that there should be so much inequality and staggering poverty. It's inarguable that we gain most of our understanding of the world through our own experiences; practical experience of what living on the streets involves would fully develop our compassion and respect for our fellow human beings.

Both governments and individuals need to consider whether the priorities in life are individual or communal. What gives the greatest good to the greater number of people, and the greatest reward? What is the purpose of spending enormous amounts of public money on one more fleet of jets, a palace or a new art gallery or two, when people in a country are suffering? For international power-posturing? Cultural snobbery? A few good-looking boulevards? The example of the credit card shows the decline in value of old-fashioned hard work and resourcefulness, as it becomes ever easier to incur debts and face the consequences later. I remember saving for months in order to buy a bicycle, while now it's nothing to 'put it on the card'. For evidence, look at the massive UK credit card debt that has been racked up in the past decades, equivalent to the combined debt of both Africa and South America! Just because we in the UK have been given the power to spend, spend, spend doesn't mean we should. A culture has sprung up of ignoring suffering, in both our own country and other parts of the world.

But this hitchhike is important to me, because I was learning that my individual wants and desires were not necessarily the be-all and end-all. Originally, I wanted merely to adventure, to reach Greece with an impressive tan and a tale in my pocket, but I was realising that not only did the world not revolve solely for my benefit, but that in fact there might be more worthwhile pastimes than simply seeking to please myself. Perhaps, I thought, I could spend my life helping others – or, even better, helping others to find compassion, empathy and humility themselves?

I arrived in Trieste on the fourth day, and was dropped off in Trieste Town Square, where I immediately collapsed onto a bench. I was too weary from lack of sleep and hunger to move, and I vividly remember chewing a loaf of bread from the day before, wondering if I was ever going to make it to Greece, as I dipped stale crusts into the remnants of a jar of blackcurrant jam. But even that poor meal was enough to pull me out of my depression, and, refreshed, I was soon on my way again.

It was mostly German tourists that stopped and occasionally offered me food – always accepted with alacrity, and a faux-casual request for water. The Dalmatian Coast was baking hot! Sitting in a metal box on those winding coastal roads, I would gaze longingly at clear emerald seas and the thousands of islands glittering amongst the waves.

Day five. I arrived in ancient Dubrovnik in the early hours. Enjoying the cool morning air, I walked around the old town walls as the city's markets were being set up. Cockerels crying out raucously in back yards mixed with the calls of market stallholders, and the sound of their rattling barrows, as they began to lay out the stalls filled with luscious, juicy fruit of every type and bright colour you could possibly imagine. Mouth watering, I dawdled past bakeries, inhaling the delicious aromas of that morning's bread, or the scent of honey and almond from a sweet shop, the sizzle of spitted meat from a street-food stand, seafood laid out on ice, offering the latest catch of squid, lobster, prawn, crab and every type of fish from the Adriatic, all tempting me. Everything in windows and market stalls was intricately arranged and laid out with care – and, from looking at the swaggering performances from stallholders, I could see that it was a daily ritual and competition between them. I had arrived in a sort of heaven of abundance here, but there was a slight snag. I had no money left. The more I walked, the more the sun beat down overhead, the more a feeling of desperation descended. I wasn't able to afford a simple peach. I was helpless. Vendors would size me up and on seeing that I was clearly not about to buy, their eyes would flick away. I was invisible. A sudden image of a London street flashed into my mind; and I saw myself wandering, dazed and scruffy, in Soho or Piccadilly, begging for money and food from everyone that passed. Here, I was just a beggar in a foreign land.

Little did I know that ten years later this beautiful city would be reduced to rubble. The founder of the charity Mary's Meals, Magnus Macfarlane Barrow, was so moved by the huge humanitarian crisis in the Balkans in the 1990s that he set up the Scottish International Relief Fund, and delivered endless truckloads of essentials to Bosnia himself. From the SIR developed Mary's Meals, a charity WildFox Events has supported on many occasions. Their purpose is to provide a decent meal for children at an educational establishment. So simple, so necessary and so effective; why are we all still so caught up in our own small daily issues when there is still the massive problem that 54 million children are without a regular meal every day?

Two other extraordinary people, brothers

Rupert and Magnus Wolfe Murray from the UK (what is it about the name Magnus?), were also deeply affected by news of this crisis, so much so that they volunteered to drive out to Romania themselves. While driving in aid agency convoys, they saw for themselves the horrifying situations in Romanian orphanages, and decided to move to Romania in order to take action by renovating orphanages. Through their love and passion, they have improved the lives of hundreds. Magnus now heads the Department For International Development in Nepal and Rupert travels the world as a travel writer and journalist.

Often, just one snap decision to make a difference can affect the paths of many different lives – not just your own! Like a tiny acorn turning into an oak, a single seed of hope can inspire thousands and set them on an entirely new way. These three exemplary men have found their purpose, and, through it, great reward.

But in 1982, all I could think about was what I could do to eat. Could I work for someone, somehow? Clean dishes? Sweep pavements? It's times like this, when one is reduced to the most fundamental resources, that one is forced to think outside the box, gather together all one's natural charm and initiative, and make the most of skills and experience... but I have to admit that in this case I failed miserably. I left that Paradisiacal jewel of a city with my tail firmly between my legs; hungry, exhausted and cross. Just one juicy peach would have been a triumph! Oh, well. Back to the drawing board.

Fast-forward to the massive refugee crisis caused by the Syrian conflict that is still rumbling on. Thousands of people are fleeing for their lives, enduring conditions much worse than I ever did on my European travels. Imagine starvation, exhaustion, dehydration, disease, cholera, rape, violence, unwelcoming reception, total, raw panic. Then imagine, on top of all this, you're caring for several small children. How can anyone imagine the horrors and tribulations of being a refugee unless they have actually experienced the nightmare? The simple answer is that we cannot. Far easier to brush it under the carpet, read the latest ghastly story of drownings in the Mediterranean and then put aside the paper, to carry on with our lives. We all care, but we do not know how to help with such overwhelming distress and mass disruption of lives. Look at me, an isolated teenager unable to barter for a piece of fruit – in a desperate predicament, yet in comparison to Syrian refugees I really had no cause to feel sorry for myself. I had two more days of going-without and then I was reckoning on being in Greece, able to look forward to borrowing money from a friend, hang out on the beach, and then catch a bus back to London. We need perspective and empathy outside our own small wants and needs: many people do not have the choices we have in the West, even if we feel hard done-by.

I was lucky to catch a lift from the outskirts of Dubrovnik from a cheery German family in a Volkswagen campervan. With one thing on my mind – food – this van was the jackpot! They had bags full of delicious goodies that I managed to relish a large portion of before being dropped off at the next town. Soon I was on my own again hitching towards Skopje, the Macedonian Capital. My next lift was not so cheery, as the passenger of some nutter with a death wish. Never, before or since, have I experienced such a terrifying hour in a car – apart from driving with my good friend Virendra Anand in the Great Desert Himalayan Car Ralley (since cancelled due to the soaring rate of fatalities)! Was this stranger who picked me up showing off to me, his unfortunate victim, or was this the normal way of driving in Macedonia? Maybe there was a family crisis, I will never know? We screeched round every hairpin bend – and there were many, descending the Macedonian Mountains – the car straining to stay on the road. What was the point of driving so fast to arrive at the destination five minutes earlier? Why are humans always in such a mad rush all the time? It was a huge relief when we arrived in Skopje and I was able to escape from the maniac. I was about to enter Greece, the final hurdle in my adventure across Europe!

A couple of lifts later I had crossed the Greek border and was heading for Thessaloniki and the road to Athens. By this time I was ravenous, not having eaten properly for three days. The latest car dropped me off at a trucker cafe at the side of the road, where, highly dramatically and literally on bended knee, I offered to wash dishes in return for food. To my delight, the waitress found me amusing and went to speak to the kitchen, after which a huge plate of spaghetti was placed in front of me with tomato sauce and meatballs. Oh, bliss! Never had a plate of spag bol tasted so good. I wolfed it down and then rolled up my sleeves heading towards the kitchen. No sooner had I begun to wash the dishes when the taverna's owner informed me that a driver was about to leave for Athens. Thanking him for his generosity, I jumped on the truck. As the driver's English was non-existent and my Greek even worse, we could communicate only through sign language. The taverna owner had told me we might stop for a rest in the early hours, and that I should get out when the driver stopped. Sure enough after six hours of driving we pulled over and I hopped out, imagining that we would be on our way again in a hour or so. Rolling out my faithful straw mat and settling down in the long grass beside the road, I thought proudly how well I had done to get so far. Soon I would be in Athens and then onto the Corinth Canal... I was rudely awoken as I was drowsing off by the engine revving – the trucker had started up and was driving away! Obviously a miscommunication somewhere. I slept well.

One more lift the following morning on Day Seven and then I arrived, in early morning heat, in Athens. Still penniless, I had to keep moving and hitched a lift with a massive steel truck heading west to the Corinth Peninsula. The seaside village of Kiatos eventually located, I headed for the beach to wait for my friend, only to discover him there, surrounded by beautiful girls. I set up camp on the beach and lived off apricots for a week, before Julian lent me enough money to return home.

What an adventure. Many lessons knocked into me with great force, but looking back thirty years later, I wonder what is it that gives people so much confidence in their own personal vision? After twenty-one lifts and seven days, I had made it to Greece, with only £40, no back-up plan, no contingency for emergency, no language skills, and indeed no base knowledge of the countries I was travelling through. Let alone a mobile phone or credit card! It was my first mad challenge, including deprivation, being homeless, hope, endurance, humility, faith in fellow human beings, a lesson in learning to do without, begging, empathy-building, compassion for those that do without on a regular basis, and a fair drumming-in of initiative.

Recalling this journey now, I do not see it

as a simple trek from A to B. It is a jumble of sensations: cobbled alleyways, the pain of sunburnt ears as I waited in the midday glare on a highway, the scent of salt wafting off a fishing boat, aching ankles after hours of standing, dark eyes which held mine as I begged for a lift. The particular places I passed through have seen much change over the past 40 years, as Europe grows, suffers, develops.

The Balkans, for example, have since moved to a relative degree of peace; other places have become sites of conflict and desperation which were, in 1982, ordinary towns and villages. One of the people I most admire is my remarkable young cousin, Ciara Connell, who has spent the last three years working with women and children refugees in the Calais Jungle which has now shifted to Dunkirk since the French destroyed it in 2016. The Dunkirk Refugee Women's Centre support women and children in these Godforsaken camps; women who suffer rapes, violence, persecution from the French police (who periodically swoop on the camps to confiscate inhabitants' belongings, shelters and backpacks as deterrents to others) in their desperate flight from war-torn countries. Ciara risks her own safety on a daily basis in order to ensure these families have food, clothing, shelter, love and support. What does it take for a nineteen-year-old to have such extraordinary compassion, personal courage and conviction, a burning urge to take direct action in order to make a difference in the lives of so many desperate people? Ciara is a volunteer and when she runs out of money returns to the UK where she finds work in order to earn money so that she can return to the Camps to continue her work of love. Ciara has a burning sense of loyalty and responsibility and she worries that if she does not continue this work, who else will? How many lives has Ciara affected? How many desperate refugees have had their lives and fortunes changed as a result of Ciara's compassion? An extraordinary person who deserves all the support she can get.

Beginning this hitchhike, I was driven by entirely the wrong reasons. I was naïve, determined and proud. I assumed that I could keep going powered by sheer arrogance and my own desire to show how tough I could be. By the end of the seven days, I had learnt a little of what purpose should truly involve.

In life, even the best-laid plans go awry. We are often blind to everything except our own desires; but one cannot expect to succeed in a singular purpose without anything getting in the way on our chosen path – whether that path is a European motorway or a less literal 'path'. We are often forced to rely on external help, as I learned on this hitchhike, and must negotiate unexpected difficulties as we cross the paths and lives of other people. Sheer determination didn't mean I'd necessarily reach my destination!

Having a strong sense of purpose involves learning humility and compassion. Commit to your goals, but notice how those goals fit into the world that surrounds you. Try to have true compassion for other people: you can't ride roughshod over them in pursuit of selfish ideals, and you'll need them – recognise that nothing can be done without love and support from those that have gone before you. Accept that however excited you are by your grand designs, things might not always go smoothly. Compromise: don't fall into the trap of mistaking 'resolve' for 'arrogance'.

But I don't want to sound too negative. I believe that everyone's life is improved when they find their purpose and are fuelled by passion. In their future careers, I hope that my own three children will do what they love and are inspired to do, not what they feel is normal – or even realistic! I'll end this chapter by telling you that, however you get there, succeeding in your chosen purpose is the best and most rewarding feeling in the world.

POINTS FOR REFLECTION

- What is our purpose, the reason for our existence?

- The question to ask yourself is this. If life would let you attempt to do something that you knew would not fail, what would it be?

- Arouse the mind, be inspired – the mind is your most powerful tool.

- No problem can withstand the assault of sustained thinking.

- Thinking is easy but acting is difficult, and to put one's thoughts into action is the most difficult thing in the world.

- Procrastination is the biggest cause of failure.

- I always wanted to be somebody but I should have been more specific.

- Do the thing and you shall have power.

- If your actions inspire others to dream more, learn more, do more and become more you are a leader.

- Everyone has their own gift from God – set an amazing target or goal and break it down into stages. Sometimes the goal as a whole can seem overwhelming.

- What can we do to improve the lives of ourselves, our families and others? Remember we can only help others once we have helped ourselves.

- With purpose comes resourcefulness and action.

- How can we kick-off our dream *now*, even if we begin in a small way?

- You must know what you want.

- Three Key Steps:
  Believe and realise that you have the power.
  Have 100% confidence in what you want.
  Concentrate your thoughts upon your plan with singular purpose.
  If you are willing to go forward and endure the mental discipline of mastering this method, nothing in the world can hinder you or keep you from overcoming every obstacle.

CHAPTER 2
PATIENCE – NEW ZEALAND VOLCANO SURVIVAL

Patience: knowing when to wait,
and when to seize the moment.

So, what next? Even once you've discovered your purpose, sometimes you have to wait until the moment is right. In this chapter I'll talk to you about patience. Patience struck me as an essential ingredient on the path to success when I became stranded in a blizzard on a volcano in New Zealand.

Heart pounding in my throat, I struggled to untie my tightly-knotted survival bag. The blizzard – straight from the Antarctic – was intensifying and my numb fingers felt like a bunch of rubber sausages. I was castigating myself for my stupidity in not turning back from this solitary hike earlier. Idiot, idiot. I'd thought I was so brave, battling uphill through the snow to complete the summit, but in fact I'd been arrogant, and had misjudged my path. I was yet to reach the top, and now it was getting dark. I seemed to hear the amused voice of my grandfather ringing in my ears. Why didn't you turn back earlier, you silly arse? But though I certainly felt like a lost little boy, there was no parent or grandparent to lift me out of this one. It was too late: a blizzard had descended, darkness was falling and I was stuck here, alone on the side of a freezing volcano.

I was beginning to understand how easy it is for people to die when hiking on mountains. They are lulled into a sense of self-congratulatory security while the weather's fine – then it turns and they're ill-prepared, and miles from civilisation. Would my equipment see me through the next twelve, fourteen, eighteen hours? I was well prepared and had most of my army kit from my parachute regiment days including enough emergency rations for 24 hours, however I had never had to test it – or myself – in such extreme conditions. What if the volcano erupted? It had last erupted a few years ago. I remembered being slumped on the National Trust Information Hut's sofa, watching lava pouring down the mountain on a fuzzy VHS. I tried to slow my rapid breathing. Now was not the time to panic. What would my parents say if I didn't make my sister's wedding?

I had stopped for literally two minutes to catch my breath and check on my location, having ascended what seemed like a very narrow ridge skirting the volcano's crater. Naively, I hadn't checked how much further I had to travel around the ridge before descending when ominous black clouds closed over the sky and the blizzard set in. In seconds, visibility was zero. As I stood there, bewildered, something strange started to happen. A perverse lethargic sense began creeping over me, a sort of laissez-faire resignation. Something in my head whispering, this is probably the best place you'll find to stop and have a rest. Just a short rest. I'd never felt the first stages of hypothermia before. My brain was shutting down and retracting the ability to think rationally. I felt truly, weirdly relaxed. Luckily, at this point I recognised something was wrong and snapped out of it. I starting barking orders to myself like my old commanders in the Parachute Regiment: get the sleeping bag out, NOW. Find the Gore-Tex bag, grab the water, baked beans and corned beef, get into the sleeping bag. Try to remember what they told you to do in an emergency, though you weren't listening, were you? I jumped up and down trying to generate heat until my heart was humming with the exertion and I could pause to look for a suitable location in which to hunker down. Banana fingers couldn't open the rucksack. Swearing, trying again, at last aggression prevailed and I snatched my four-seasons sleeping bag, stuffed it into my bivvy bag and jumped in, boots and all. There was little shelter on offer, only a large boulder which I wedged myself beside out of the blizzard, zipping myself into my bag, including my head.

So. Here I was, in a worrying predicament, to say the least. I had been enjoying my last few days of backpacking in New Zealand before the return to Scotland for my sister's wedding in seven days time. I was cramming two days into each one, seeing as much as possible before my departure from the Southern Hemisphere – possibly for ever, who knew? And then I had to get myself into a pickle like this. At this rate the wedding on the 27th of July would be followed by a family funeral. It was 5pm, pitch dark now, New Zealand winter time. This was a part of the world notorious for long-lasting vicious storms, which swooped in from the Antarctic with little warning. I'd heard about them from the brief research I'd done before beginning this trip. Was this one of these monsters? I combed my memory, but I was sure there'd been no mention of the storm when I had checked into the National Park Office at the start of my walk... Again I recalled the music at the Trust Office and watching the standard video on volcanic activity: a cheery narrator telling me: 'What goes up must come down'. Well, I was heading up and I certainly hoped they were right on that one.

Now that I was stationary in the bag, I knew I had to generate heat – and fast. My heart was still pounding in its cardiac efforts to warm my vitals. I started frantically punching at the inside of my bag, and gradually, my temperature began to normalise. I tore open the baked beans and drank them, clawing out corned beef from its tin with my hands, to wolf down with a swig of water. Amazing what nutrition does to the body temperature, even when the food is stone icy cold. Having eaten, I now had nothing to distract me from what faced me: the longest night of my life. The kit I had would have to see me through this ordeal. Suddenly, a queer excitement kicked in, (admittedly mixed with fear, trepidation and anxiety). This was the ultimate adventure. After all, what had all the training in the Parachute Regiment (TA) been for, if not for this? Thank God I had packed the breathable Gore-Tex survival bag. This was a real life-saver, a piece of kit that I had used on exercise with the regiment a few years back. I racked my brains: when had I last tested this kit in extreme weather? It was back in my Parachute Regiment days, those miserable nights training in the Scottish Glens and patrolling in the winter in minus temperatures (well, I'd thought it was tough at that time. Now, however...). It was back in the Parachute Company at Aldershot, where I spent two weeks in the field under intense physical endurance tests, or rather, torture: ten-mile battle marches, log and stretcher races, assault courses, 'milling' (boxing), parachuting from balloons and then Hercules c130 Aircraft... night jumps, day jumps, water jumps, jumps with full kit and rifle, river crossing with full kit, weapons training, live-firing exercises, Exercise Lionheart in Germany – the biggest combined NATO training exercise since World War II. A good general all-rounder in the school of toughening up!

But all that time, I had been alongside my fellow soldiers. I just did not know if all this training and roughing it around the world had been any more than Boy Scout play-fighting. I did not know if I could simply survive alone for eight more hours.

I had not seen a soul all day on the mountain. That was fine; I had been travelling alone around the world over the past six months. On your own, you are more approachable and people are more likely to strike up a conversation. I still firmly believe that the general experience of the single traveller is more diverse and enriching than travelling in a group – you are less likely to interact with strangers in the same way.

Being alone on this volcano was a different type of 'alone'. No-one was coming my way, at least until someone had discovered my absence. Even then, that might take two, three or four days. Alone as I was, acutely feeling a proximity to death, I felt suddenly aware that I was at the total and utter mercy of a power outside of myself. Nature, God, an omnipotent force. Was this a test, and if it was, how could I pass? Should I even want to? I quickly put this thought out of my mind. I was too young to die. I was only twenty-three, and though unsure about many things, I fervently believed in some kind of higher being. Whether one calls this the power of the Universe, 'God' or positive thought is a different matter. As I huddled in the snow, I couldn't help thinking how pointless it seemed to go to church and mumble over the same words again and again, begging for absolution and forgiveness of our sins. Looking down my nose to stare death in the face, it seemed that a more practical approach, doing something to make a difference in support of the many desperate people on this planet, might, for me, be a more constructive way of practicing my faith.

I was pulled out of my philosophical considerations by extraordinary rocking sensations which started to occur, making me feel like a fly suspended in an enormous, swaying spiderweb. Every ten minutes or so there came a weird swooshing sound, approaching and crescendoing like a freight train roaring to reach a frightening pitch before dying down. This must have been the wind and snow rushing around the crater at hundreds of miles an hour – and here I was, perched on the highest part of the crater's Western ridge, partially sheltered by a rock! Yet my thoughts were free to roam, and leapt wildly about, from the people who mattered to me, to the places I had been and how I felt about them. It seems time paused then, or stretched hundred-fold. What had I lived for, now I had the time to think about it? I dissected my life, family, friends, girlfriends, my exploring, the countries I'd visited, my time in Hong Kong, experiences. Travels. Adventures. While I was wedged against that ridiculous rock, I thought in particular of my grandfather, who had recently died aged 95. A founding member of the Welsh Guards, he'd fought in two World Wars. I felt pretty pathetic in comparison.

I had arrived in Perth, Western Australia three months earlier, with just £10 to my name. This was before the credit card-mobile phone era, and anyway, I was too stubborn to ask for money from my parents. They had always expected me to find work – no such thing as pocket money in our household! I'd done lots of low-paid jobs while I scrabbled for a wage: farm labouring, tatty-picking and driving tractors, before saving enough to embark on a hotel management course. This early lesson in self-resilience stood me in good stead, and the day after arriving from Asia I'd checked into an agricultural job agency in Perth. The first opportunity to come up was as a tractor driver and farm labourer on a remote farm near Grass Patch, Esperance, a six-hour drive south from Perth. I snatched at the chance and headed south on a bus to Esperance – borrowing money off the agent to pay the bus fare. For the next two months, my days consisted of long sessions driving a massive Versatile Canadian Tractor, ploughing, sowing, and hours spent stacking the many bush stumps that the ploughing unearthed. I lived in a caravan in the barn and rose at 6am to start work, eating a packed lunch on the tractor, with dinner brought out to me at 6pm. Richard, my boss, relieved me at midnight. He'd keep the beast rolling till 6am, and then I was back in the seat. When the rains fell we had to go all out to prepare the land before the ground became too hard. I remembered the large artificial ponds for farming of 'scabbies' (shrimps); chasing lambs for 'muelsing' (tail cutting); and supporting the teams of Kiwi shearers on their long rounds. They were tough people, travelling the miles and miles between these remote farms during shearing season. I remember being so impressed with the resourcefulness of the farmers I met, and with how much Richard and I accomplished alone. It was an alien environment indeed, making eight-hour Scottish shifts (with constant tea breaks) seem rather half-hearted in comparison. The job came to an end, having earned me enough money to continue on my journey towards New Zealand... in blissful innocence of what was coming to me, I thought grimly on my exposed crater edge, tucking my hands further into my armpits.

I got the news that my paternal grandfather had died while working on the Australian farm. That was the clearest memory, of course: I had been attempting to repair the seeder in the tool shed with a large rusty spanner, trying desperately to loosen a nut when the spanner slipped, whacking me on the head. Reeling back in agony, my grandfather's face suddenly sprang before my mind's eye. I learnt later that it was at this exact moment that he had died, 10,000 miles away. Billy Fox-Pitt joined up to fight in World War I when he was seventeen. He joined first the Sherwood Foresters and then the Cheshire Regiment. Both were decimated before 1915. He then became a founder members of the Welsh Guards, was wounded on several occasions in the trenches, sometimes returning to England before being sent back out to the Front. He survived all the friends of his youth, then went on to fight another World War. He retired as a Major General and died at 95. He was given a full regimental guard of honour for his send-off in Sherborne Abbey. I was enormously proud of him and respected him more than anyone I knew. It was as if he was sending me a final message: old boy, I'm off, now make something of your life. I hadn't – I was gambling with it for no good reason except the folly of youth as I fought for my life on this blizzard-blasted mountain.

Every man is guilty of all the good he did not do, and I was feeling this painfully right now. How many of us regret all the things we have not done, especially helping those souls less fortunate than ourselves? Probably the best deeds I'd ever done had been during 1986, during my time spent with the Reverend John Warren, a Christian missionary in the Philippines. For a remarkable two months, I'd

followed John through countless villages on the remote island of Luzon, witnessing miracles. It was
like winding the clock back by two hundred years:
no washing-machines, dishwashers, cars, trains,
electricity, or any of the modern conveniences I'd
been accustomed to. The extraordinarily evocative
sights of that landscape printed themselves onto my
mind forever: buffalo and oxen slowly pulling the
plough through the myriad terraces, the bent sil-
houettes of women stooping to plant rice shoots,
pigs and chickens scratching together in the dust.
We lived in an orphanage for two weeks near Bagio. I was made a godfather to two children near
Talubin. I remembered being staggered by the
stunning Banawi rice terraces, known locally as 'the
Stairways to Heaven'. It was all a blur of bright-
ly-coloured buses, the beautiful laughter of women,
the light pearl-blue ocean and the amazing generosity, hope, and faith of all the local people we met.

Luzon in 1986 seemed very far away. It was
now 9pm, I had been in the bag for five hours, my
feet were frozen numb and the blizzard was beginning a fresh onslaught. I was also very aware of the
possibility that my Gore-Tex would freeze solid,
and so every now and then I made mad shuffling
movements, trying to shake off my cover of snow.
The rock wasn't wide enough to protect all of me
from the onslaught and the bottom half of the
sleeping bag was exposed to the storm, so my legs

were growing colder by the second, but this poor refuge was all there was. I just had to keep awake and hope that I would survive until first light. Though I tried to focus on good memories (positiverosity, David!), I could not keep disquieting thoughts from invading my mind. I thought of my mother's father, also a career soldier, who died aged 32, fighting the Germans at Anzio. He was commanding the Scots Guards and my mother was only two. His family had to live without him – and here I was, squandering my life through a stupid decision at the age of twenty-three! It was funny how this predicament brought up thoughts of my grandfathers' generation as the nearest comparison. Closest to home. We underestimate the enormous sacrifice they endured in order for us to enjoy relative peace unthinkingly today, although there is still too much fighting and aggression around the world.

Well, I'd been outdoors a lot in my short life. I had built up a considerable level of fitness in the Parachute Regiment, and used to lead long walks in the wilds of the New Territories and the multitudinous Hong Kong Islands, when I was working at the Raffles Club there. I tried to plot out the precise route of these walks, to block out rising panic. I remembered spending two months sleeping on an office floor in the Bank of America Tower where I worked, having given up my lodgings in Hong Kong to a friend in order to raise funds for an orphanage. How cold that marble floor felt through the cardboard I slept on – still, not as cold as I was now. It was great for my back and my bank account (lodgings being very expensive in Hong Kong) and it certainly built up resilience for travels yet to come... Though I certainly could never have predicted I'd need to deal with this level of cold and discomfort. My God, how was I to get out? I swore I'd be grateful for any kind of sleeping mat in the future, give me a sheet of cardboard on an office floor in the sweltering tropics any time.

I had now been in the survival bag for seven hours and it was almost midnight. Such a weird sensation, being inside the Gore-Tex bag. What was going on out there? The mountain was driving me mad. It was playing mind games with me. The whoosh of the freight train and the suspended spider theme replaying, over and over. Never had I appreciated the human power of imagination so much. My mind just about ran riot with crazy scenarios. What would happen if this volcano did go off? Would I just rip the bag off and run for it? Would I stay where I was and hope for the best? Would I get sucked down into the crater? I had been walking through thick murky clag of a fog all day and had little idea of my surroundings. If the storm died down, could I make a run for it? Would my torch be bright enough to see through the blizzard, or would I just slide down off the rim and into the crater? It had been icy most of the way up, I imagined the crater would be full of ice. Once I had slipped down into the depths of its cauldron I'd never be discovered, making my chances of attending my sister's wedding even less. I would not give up. I was determined not to spoil it for everyone.

What would my family be up to, right now? It was the height of British summer on the other side of the world. I imagined my mother going through the wedding plans and seating arrangements for dinner. Guests, pageboys, and bridesmaids would be preparing to invade Perthshire. They were rehearsing in Dunkeld Cathedral on Friday. Dinner and dancing were to be held at the stunning Blair Castle, home of the Duke of Atholl. It was incredibly frustrating to think of dying without being able to at least speak to someone and say my farewells! I had been in the bag for seven hours already and had at least until first light, to survive. Eight hours away, I estimated. I would then dash back in the direction I came and make my way down to one of the refuge huts I had walked past the day before. I just needed to get through the next eight hours. Shake that ice off the bag, keep moving, keep positive, keep motivated, keep alert, keep planning my exit strategy but above all keep calm, hold my nerve, be patient and wait it out.

Thinking of my sister reminded me of the

beginning of this now-godawful journey. Five months ago, in a balmy January, I'd set off to a four-day wedding extravaganza in Delhi – a wonderful start to my travels. Virendra, a very good friend from Hong Kong, was getting married and this had been the catalyst to my round-the-world trip. The first couple of days were spent visiting all the relations, eating feast after feast with family after family. Hmm, I could do with one of those feasts right now. It was a huge honour to be included as a relative, and a remarkable insight into the Hindu religion for me. Dressed up in a traditional red turban for the big day, I'd joined the initial service at Virendra's house, and then the fun started. We were stuffed into a convoy of cars, which threw us out about a mile from the wedding venue, in front of a live band of musicians. We then danced to the wedding, frantically zigzagging down the streets of Delhi. I could conjure up the colours: pink, red, gold; the noise of hooting horns and laughter, the wailing music and the heat of exhaust fumes. What a stark contrast to my current position, I thought, watching my breath condense on the interior of the bivvy bag. Almost the complete opposite, in fact. We arrived sweating at the venue, a massive marquee, and shortly afterwards the wedding ceremony proper started. Both the bride and groom were very solemn, certainly not looking as if they were enjoying themselves. The Hindu priest ran through his rituals, with seven rotations round the firepit at the centre of the tent. It was sweltering. Was poor Virendra actually upset, or was it customary to look that miserable? After the service, one wall suddenly rolled up to reveal a whole other part to the marquee where a lavish buffet was laid out. On cue the guests descended like locusts, stripped the tables of food and left. Virendra and his wife sat on a raised stage, encased in magnificent glittering robes. Every now and then one of the women would approach Virendra and thrust cake into his mouth, apparently irritating him immensely. If this was the tradition, I supposed he had to put up with it. The party continued at Claridges in Delhi well into the early hours, and we eventually retired after a monumentally fun day. A day I shall never forget, a day that was now providing me with many fond recollections with which to pass the hours of this ordeal.

2am. Nine hours in the sack. The storm had not abated; if anything, it seemed to have picked up. Again, this could be my hysterical imagination. Was that numbness creeping up my legs, in the early stages of frostbite? Even if not, I had to keep my legs moving, generate heat, not fall asleep. How could I do something about the blizzard? It drove me mad to know that I could do nothing. There were no options, I had chosen the best spot I could find and that was that. Get on and make the best of it.

After the wedding in Delhi, I bid farewell

to Virendra, and his incredibly generous and kind family – a second family, to me. Virendra is a true and loyal friend, but unlike my scary hitchhiking experiences, I trusted Virendra's driving completely and I'd later put my life in his hands during the Great Desert Himalayan Car Rally. I bought a bus ticket to Srinagar, Kashmir and endured a twenty-five hour hell-raiser of a journey, driving at breakneck speed through the Punjab Province. The driver paused to put on a turban for the Punjab section of the drive, and afterwards refused to stop.

It was well known that in previous weeks Hindu passengers had been ordered off buses and straight away beheaded. These were worrying times. Indira Ghandi had been assassinated a few months earlier by her Sikh Guards over the Golden Temple storming in Amritsar. However, a more immediate problem for me was how the bus managed to stay on the road. No barriers, massive drops either side of the mountainous road, the continuous use of the wretched horn, recently cleared landslides, loud, tinny Hindu music, what one might kindly call a 'rich variety' of smells, and a thick layer of dust covering everything. The driver seemed to be on some weed-driven, obsessed, aggressive pilgrimage himself, and his ultimate Holy Grail was Srinagar! No doubt, it was a nail-biting experience, but at the same time an adventure, and my first introduction to the maniac driving styles of the subcontinent. We passed by twenty severe crashes and wrecks on that twenty-five hour journey; I was constantly reminded of the consequences when things went wrong.

Things going wrong... the time was now approaching 5am and I was beginning to see a glimmer of light at the end of the tunnel. Perhaps I could get through this, perhaps this amazing Gore-Tex bag was actually going to save my life. I had spent twelve hours in this position now, and it would be getting light in just three more. I started to rehearse my exit plan. I would jump out of the bag, gracefully and rapidly scoop everything into the rucksack, then make a dash for it down the ridge. Ideal! However, there was a possibility that I was not going to be able to walk: I had no feeling in my legs below the knee. Also, there were no signals from my bladder, even though I had been drinking through the night – an ominous sign of severe dehydration...

Quick, what next? Srinagar! Srinagar, the Venice of the East, a town lying in an extraordinary position in the Kashmir Valley between the frozen Dal and Anchar lakes. Famous for its ancient Mughal Gardens: Chashma Shahi (the Royal Fountains), Pari Mahal (the Palace of the Fairies), Nishat Bagh (the Garden of Spring), and, of course, the Shalimar Gardens; one of the wonders of the world. I adored the outfits in the crammed and humming bazaars, and bought for myself a tweed Sherlock Holmes-style cloak – ideal for the colonial civil servant, keeping me warm during cold Kashmir nights. The busy people all seemed to be carrying something under their cloaks. Their hunched, cloaked stance perplexed me until I worked out they were holding little clay pots of heated coals to keep them warm – just like the stone hot water bottles we had in Perthshire! I spent a couple of nights on a longboat on one of the lakes, explored the lush gardens of the maharajahs, and was fortuitously drawn into a local game of cricket. Passing by, the game caught my eye and I paused to watch from the boundary, when the batsman smacked the ball for a six directly towards me. I stepped forward, time seemed to slow, and the ball plopped into my waiting hands just short of the line. A sweet sound, followed by an equally gratifying cheer from the fielding team, and a less welcome roar of fury from the batting team protesting at this foreign intruder interfering in their game... things could have become a little touchy, but all was cleared up by them simply adding me to the fielding team. We then played one of the most enjoyable games of cricket ever experienced by mankind, in the surroundings of the beautiful old Mughal town.

From Srinagar, I travelled close to the border of Pakistan, to a remote ski village called Gulmarg. The Indian Army was out in force on the slopes, ominously camped but not actually skiing. I was apparently the only skier there, and spent a freezing night in cheap accommodation before making an executive decision to head back to Srinagar. One week later the region was hit by terrible avalanches that killed many people, including a great friend of Prince Charles.

Enough of distracting myself. Finally, first light was approaching, and I must gather my wits, be canny about it. I was going to make a run for it. Twelve hours in the bag, and I was desperate. The storm had not, however, showed any signs of abating, and I was not sure what I would face outside... but surely, it was time. I unzipped the bivvy bag, smashing the ice that had formed on it, and half-wriggled, half-jumped out, my feet numb from lying down for so long. Within seconds I was even colder than I had been before, my deadened fingers useless as I tried to prod my things into the rucksack.

Wind screaming in my ears, I swung the rucksack high on my back and scrambled downhill, but was blown off the ridge almost immediately, and had to scrabble for my life back up the ridge and back to my faithful boulder. It was not going to work, the storm was in full flow and it was too risky to break out. Within two minutes I was back in the bag, tearful with desperation and praying with all my heart for a break in the storm. Back to square one, heart rate back to manic mode and freezing cold. What a waste of energy. This time I was really at risk: there was no food left apart from a couple of biscuits and all I could do was hunker down and wait.

I thought of everything I had been thinking about for the past twelve hours. I had done plenty in my life: I had loved people, worked, travelled... I had been lucky. Yet I still felt there was so much to do. For me, it had become clear: I wanted to make a concrete difference to other peoples' lives. First, I must attend that wedding of my sister's and spend longer with my family. It was at that point I realised that so many people forget to fulfil themselves in life. They battle through life feeling dissatisfied and hating what they do. Why is this the case? Fear of the unknown, fear of failure, of looking stupid, being different? But is it better to be a sheep than to be wrong? Now, faced with a pointless death on the side of a volcano, I realised that living life – rather than letting life make your decisions for you – is a choice. Failure means nothing in comparison to never trying at all. I promised myself if I ever got out of this mess I would never again fear failure. I would not just experience life; I would create my life and I would make a difference in other people's lives.

Midday, eighteen hours in the sack, and I was slipping into hypothermia. I have to do something, I thought, for the umpteenth time. Time was running out. By now, my legs had lost all feeling and my hands and arms were also going. There was no choice, I had to break out, before the last of my will deserted me.

For the second time I struggled out of my bag, crammed it into the rucksack, blood instantly icing in my veins. Hunched close to the ground this time, dragging the rucksack behind me, I staggered down the ridge. Though the cold and biting wind was agonising, it was a huge relief to be moving. This time there was no going back to the boulder. Neon-red marker poles loomed up and disappeared every now and then against the swirling grey, pointing me on the right path as I descended – every one a heavenly sight, confirming that I was retracing my steps correctly. As I moved slowly onwards, gradually, my body started to thaw out. At first I felt a slight tingling in my feet, arms and legs, and then dull aching as my blood warmed. I felt an extraordinary sense of overwhelming joy. Every step was a step towards new life. I had been given a second chance. I was going to make my sister's wedding. I was going to look at my life in a different light – make something of it, and give something back.

Eventually I reached the refuge hut I had passed twenty hours earlier on my way up the mountain. My energy levels were now completely depleted: I was lasting on borrowed time. Stumbling into the hut, I shut the door on the storm. Firewood! But my hopes were dashed when I pulled out the matches from my rucksack – they were sodden, and I was not going to start rubbing sticks together. Though

I was ravenously hungry, I had no food, and barely any energy to think. All I could do was pull my sleeping bag over me and I was out like a light. I cannot remember ever sleeping for so long and so well.

I stayed in the refuge hut for a further sixteen hours, before eventually gathering my resources and leaving that mountain for the last time. I managed to hitch a lift with a trucker into the local town. Recounting my sorry story to the driver, it began to dawn on me how lucky I had been to survive. He confirmed that the storm had been a bad one. Locals were used to hearing of ill-prepared tourists dying on the mountainside, caught out when the weather turns. The friendly trucker dropped me off at the local supermarket, where I filled my basket with as much of my favourite food as I could carry. I treated myself to a B&B for one more night before heading back to the safety of Auckland and the UK.

It may seem strange to write about patience and on the same page urge you to fearless action. I believe they are two sides of the same coin. Knowing when to seize the moment is part of the patient waiting. Those hours I spent in a bivvy bag, during which I was forced to take the time to consider my life, gave me perspective. They helped me see that patience is not about hanging around waiting for life to happen to you; it is about stepping back and considering what it is you really want – and then working, working, working to get it. It may take a long time, and much effort. Remember, the end point of patience is taking action.

What is the definition of a good and fulfilled life? Happiness, love, fulfilment and recognition seem to be high on the agenda as a way to a successful life. My definition is simple. To be fulfilled you must be passionate about what you do in life. We are only on the planet for a few years: we need to make the most of it. Enjoy it – we may as well.

POINTS FOR REFLECTION

- There are moments when everything goes well, but don't be frightened, it won't last – prepare for the ups and downs of life.

- If you want to set an example, try patience, for it is often perceived as genius.

- Look deep into nature and you will understand everything better.

- Waste no tears over the griefs of yesterday.

- Know your equipment well and judge the most appropriate time to strike out in adversity.

- Have faith in a higher being – The Universe, Nature, God, whatever you deem to be a higher being.

- Always have faith and belief that you will prevail and succeed, come what may.

- Test your patience by being the last one to leave the plane. If you have time, always let others go first.

- Show humility and do not antagonise. Show interest in other people, ask them about themselves, learn from them and listen to them with a smile.

- Remember that success can be a long game. Always plan for the long haul.

- Know and trust yourself so that in times of trial you can provide comfort and reassurance to others.

- Never send harsh e-mails, sleep on it and re-appraise before you press that button.

- Count to ten before reacting. Never loose your temper and try to avoid conflict.

- Anger is a wind which blows out the lamp of the mind.

- You cannot shake hands with a clenched fist.

- If you have a dispute with someone make peace with them before the sun goes down.

CHAPTER 3
PRACTICALITY – CHRISTIAN MISSIONARY IN THE PHILIPPINES, DECEMBER 1986

Practical faith and belief: the ignition for and inspiration behind supporting humanitarian work.

Practicality means putting your passion into practice. When I joined a Christian missionary in the Philippines, I became enlightened as to how thinking in practical terms is a vital part of achieving your goals.

When I touched down on the runway, although I didn't know it then, it was one of those moments when a new chapter of your life begins.

I was joining The Reverend John Warren, the uncle of one of my oldest friends, in his vocation as a Christian Missionary in the Philippines. Tim Warren and I had worked together in Palm Beach Florida at the Breakers Hotel on a hotel management course and later set up a venue-finding business for conferences which Tim still runs. Tim is a highly positive individual with an extraordinarily creative mind and exceptional positive spirit. I didn't know his uncle John well myself, as he had been supporting communities in these islands for over ten years, and lived mainly in the Northern Island of Luzon. I had no idea what to expect, joining him as a volunteer, or even what exactly my four weeks in the country would entail. I had just got a job in Hong Kong as a manager of Raffles, an exclusive private membership club in the middle of central Hong Kong, and had agreed to help John for a month before that, as a stop-off before Hong Kong. It seemed convenient and likely to be of interest. I didn't know just how much this experience would change me.

I was flying in from Palm Beach, Florida, having just completed a twelve-month Hotel Management course there. I had spent over one year in one of the richest towns in America, at a luxury hotel which catered for the most pampered of clientele, and here I was heading back to a country whose main industry was farming! My friends in Florida thought it was ludicrous, but to me it was a natural progression. All my time in Florida, I had been desperate for exoticism, excitement, travel. Ideally, I wanted to use my training as a hotelier somewhere tropical and exciting, so the hotel job in Hong Kong was what I'd dreamed of – but why had I also felt the need to take John up on his offer of voluntary work? I didn't have an evidently strong Christian faith or previous interest in the Philippines. Was it purely for the adventure? No. There was something else about it that appealed to me, when I made the decision in Florida. I had everything I needed there, and would in Hong Kong... and yet something about the vision of a basic way of life, free from materialism and close to nature appealed to me. It was going to be an adventure.

My first few days after touchdown were spent in an orphanage near a small town called Bagio. This was John's base: from here he planned all trips to the hard-to-reach, mountainous interior of the country. It was 1987, and the notoriously corrupt President Ferdinand Marcos had recently been overthrown as military dictator. Imelda, his wife, was infamous for gathering over 6000 pairs of shoes – shocking, for the wife of a politician, but predictable in a country with huge disparity between rich and poor.

My first trip was to the northern island of Luzon, by bus. Although I had no idea of our route, or what our plan was, John seemed to have a circuit that he followed on an annual basis and he would visit communities all over the island. Even now, when arriving anywhere, I mentally compare my reception with the welcoming committees on this first trip. Hundreds of children crowded the bus before we could get off, screaming and giggling, fascinated by these strange, tall, white 'ghosts' with long noses! (After constant comments, I became very self-conscious about the size of my nose). It was the first time – not the last – I experienced the feeling of racial alienation in another country, and I began to realise a little of what it felt like to look different to the others around you, to be in a minority. Of course, I can never fully understand the systematic discrimination against minorities that occurs in my own and other countries, but I believe the experience of standing out, being judged by the colour of your skin, is a practical experience that has helped me. In Europe and the USA, it is all to easy to ignore our privileges; here, we looked and attracted considerable attention.

Our visit to a village would always start off in the same way: tea, coffee and a general catch up with the elders. This chit chat appeared to be the equivalent of tea with the vicar – I half expected to see my grandmother coming in with a plate of Mr Kipling's cakes. Eventually, after the niceties had been dispensed with, John and I would be led off to meet the sick and infirm. John would lay his hands on them and we would all pray. The whole experience reminded me of stories in the Bible about Jesus travelling around the country to heal people. Many of the areas we visited had no roads and we would walk for hours and hours to reach the villages. It was not, however, the lack of infrastructure and amenities that reminded me of Biblical times. (I think it is patronising, even insulting, to call the country 'undeveloped', or 'uncivilised'.) What reminded me of Bible stories was the way John, like Jesus, talked frankly with ordinary people on their sickbeds, soothed their everyday worries, comforted them and showed them love and respect. It was all very ordinary and practical, with exchanges of sensible advice and demonstrations of real care.

However, after our rounds of visiting various sick folk and the elderly, we would then have a church service... an entirely different experience. And rather an extraordinary one, for someone more used to the restrained Church of England. For one thing, fifty percent of the congregation would be made up of children. Not just a couple of sedate youngsters relegated to Sunday School as soon as the sermon got underway, but a huge gang crammed onto the benches and filling up the first five rows, shouting, laughing, playing and singing. Our host pastor, the Master of Ceremonies at this extravagant, exciting event, would have to roar over the top of their voices when he asked for peace, then would introduce John and I in the reverent silence that instantly followed.

After several lively hymns and songs (no solemn marches here), the religious part of the service commenced: the entire congregation would be taken over by the 'Holy Spirit'. The pastor would build the congregation up into a frenzy with chanting and wailing, while the children at the front all sat and stared devoutly at the spectacle – as well they might – as, one by one, their parents and respected elders began to sway and fall about, totally possessed by the Holy Spirit, lucky if someone caught them before they crashed onto the hard ground. Then they began bellowing all sorts of unpronounceables, speaking in tongues. I nudged John in the ribs, and goggling, hissed 'What on earth is going on?' It must have been some kind of hoax, right? John said simply, 'David, they are being consumed by the Holy Spirit'.

I wanted a more complex explanation. It just all seemed so odd! Were they falling backwards because that was what they thought they should do, or were they really being overcome by the spirit? To this day I will never know, and some part of me always dreaded that part of the service; we are all afraid of what is alien to us. What struck me most was their extraordinary faith in Jesus. When John laid his hands on the sick, they really believed they were being touched by Christ, and I saw myself how many gained the strength to recover. This type of faith is all but lost in the cynical West. If we were to regain it, would it help some of the ills of our society?

I am not a particularly spiritual man. To me, 'faith' is defined as a simple belief that good will prevail. I have seen how powerful a support faith, belief in others and ourselves, can be – in both small and larger ways. It is down to the power of positive thinking. Cycles of negative thought are self-defeating, whereas faith in divine help (as I saw in the Philippines) is the very opposite to this: it is self-belief. Unflinching faith, whether in Christianity or yourself, really can move mountains on your behalf.

The faith I saw in these village churches was so raw, so effective and so wonderful to witness in practice. The people were as loving and giving as true Christianity asks one to be. They had very little in the way of possessions, but they gave us a warm and genuine welcome, always preparing their best food (without exception, pork or chicken with rice) and treating us missionaries like long lost family members. The elderly were supported within the family home and treated with dignity. What a sharp contrast to Palm Beach! I had seen many lonely retirees and ghastly old-peoples' homes in Florida and the UK. Old folk discarded, cared for by paid strangers, with relatives too busy to see them. In the West, we are forced to prioritise money, independence and security, and often forget that the more important things in life are other people. I found it incredible, after my year in a luxury resort in which every guest and every employee was stressed about their income, that these poorer people were so generous. Because they had faith in the power of good, they valued generosity over everything.

The church service would last for probably about an hour, and then the children would be off to bed – followed shortly afterwards by their parents. (Most of the places we visited did not have electricity, so communities worked and lived by daylight. It took me some time, but I learned to love rising early with the sun when our hosts began their day tending to the animals and fields.) We'd have enjoyed a delicious dinner, eaten with the most respected people of the village (again: always the elder people), during which John and they would discuss the many concerns experienced since his last visit. Issues were typically divided into health, work and security worries. At that time, gangs roamed the remoter parts of the Philippine jungle extorting food and money off locals, so there was a higher than average concern over security. John's pastors would give their report back on all the issues. It was fascinating, learning about the complex challenges these remote communities faced, and we would sometimes chat for many hours before our hosts politely reminded us it was time for bed.

Our sleeping quarters were basic: perhaps a roll mat for a mattress, shared inevitably with fleas and mosquitos. Toilets were equally basic, but I was surprised by how clean they always were; the villages must have some particular form of waste-disposal, I assumed. However, on one trip John visited the bathroom (a 'squat and drop' above the pigpen) for a number two. The expectant pig in its designated pen below mistimed its morning catch, and was immediately coroneted. To the delight of the locals, and the extreme embarrassment of John, the children rushed around the village proclaiming that John had 'crowned the pig'! It did somehow put us off our pork dish at the next village when we discovered the way the pigs were being fed.

Farming was the main profession, and in 1987 was done mainly by hand. It was back-breakingly hard work, no romance about it. Rice paddy fields stretched as far as the eye could see, thousands and thousands all the way to the horizon. It was hypnotic to watch this centuries-old way of farming; every now and then, a pair of oxen driving a plough would pass me, kicking up sludgy mud in their slow, graceful route through the fields, the farmer calmly guiding them and murmuring instructions for the beasts' every move. For me, there was something reassuring about watching this traditional practice carrying on. It was incredibly hard, but it was honest and self-sufficient – not like the Palm Beach hotel.

Why does it often seem that we in the West have lost our way? At what point did our connection with a simple way of life start to evaporate? We have become disconnected with the cycles of nature, producing food and caring for each other in faith. Was it around the time of the Industrial Revolution, when we started to become more affluent and our work became less practically relevant to ourselves? I am writing this story sitting in my house, having just returned from a magical walk deep in the woodland on the banks of Loch Tay. Over 100 years earlier these shores would have been surrounded by similar scenes to those I witnessed in the Philippines: in our part of Scotland, the *shielings* (small Scottish crofts) lie scattered and broken throughout the Glens where once thousands of souls scratched a hard, honest living from the land. No supermarkets in those days, no public transport, no luxuries. In the Philippines I was transported back in time, back to an age I had only read about, and I was spell-bound.

Of course, I am well aware that we only yearn for things we have not got, and if we knew what we were really missing, then we would not yearn. We cannot underestimate how hard it would be to live in a society where each community depends on what it can grow. It is easy to point out the benefits of supermarkets and hot baths and yet to see the contrast in the Philippines has called to my attention what we have lost. This rapid change is affecting the whole world. The elderly people I used to talk with in the Philippines lamented that their younger relatives were moving to the cities in search of work, and they grumbled that there were no young left to tend to the fields. The same happened in Scotland during the Industrial Revolution, the countryside emptying as people moved to wealthy industrial cities or emigrated overseas to seek their fortunes. We gained, but we lost the old way of life. It's the same the world over; recently, it has been happening in booming China over the last two decades; it will always happen. I still feel there is something to be said for practical work, the peace of nature, the old ways.

I had often wondered what it would be like living without cars and mechanisation, as we all have, and here I was experiencing this wonderful part of the world which the engine had not yet reached. I felt an amazing sense of peace and calmness, time to think and not always to rush, hours walking through endless remote rural communities, observing, watching, listening and marvelling. When we reached a village, we would then be immersed in its community for 24 hours and consumed in its particular matters and problems.

I would often close my eyes to conjure up an image of home in a similar situation without engines, and I would see myself transported back in time. How have we changed since industrialisation? I can only see that we expect more, want more, are less patient, more spoilt, less caring, less sharing, greedy – and yet we still all strive for the same things. Love, attention, warmth, food, and fulfilment. In the Philippines, the communities I visited with John were at that time unaffected by industrialisation and were content without modern distractions.

I wonder how life has changed since I was there?

What was I learning during this visit back in 1987, and what impact was it having on my personal moral compass? One lesson that hit home was that people are all the same the world over, and we should not call one way of life 'civilised' or 'uncivilised'. Children are the same, in Africa, Scotland, the Philippines or China. They need to be loved by their parents, families, and communities. Children have such a fantastic sense of enthusiasm and passion for life, laughter and fun. What is it that we do as humans to destroy this innocence? What is that makes us greedy, jealous, competitive, lacking faith and wisdom and in some cases resorting to violence and drugs? There did not seem to be any violence and vices in the village communities we passed through. The children were full of joy and happiness and boundless enthusiasm. They had enormous freedom to roam and play in the villages (no cars). The communities had their faith in each other and themselves. They were forgiving and loving, as both Christianity and their previous faiths taught them to be.

One question that kept me awake at night while I was on this expedition was what right we colonisers had had to come in and preach Christianity rather than let them continue in their own beliefs. By the time I was there, the villages we visited were already Christian; nevertheless, I have no answer for this. There were also Catholic Communities and missionaries and Muslim communities, mainly in the southern islands: diversity and toleration was as much part of their religion as belief in any specific God. The very real value of all these foreign missionaries of any description was the practical reassurance they gave to the people; I felt and still feel this to this day.

Meanwhile, I personally relished the opportunity to recharge my spiritual batteries, live in a more thoughtful way and simply spend more time thinking, thinking about the future and what impact I may be able to have on this stressed world. I was lucky to have this time to focus on thinking about my passions while developing my own compassion and direction in life. One occasion I clearly remember was when we attended a service close to the Banui Rice Terraces, otherwise known as the 'Stairways to Heaven'. Rice terraces stepped high up into the mists of the mountains, vibrant green and beautifully cared for. I remember wondering how long this tradition would last if all the children preferred city life. Ten years? Twenty, if I was being generous with my estimates? That service was particularly packed out with several children attending to be confirmed. To my utmost surprise, I was asked to be the godfather of two children – I was most honoured. I hadn't realised that my work, and my company, was so appreciated by the parents.

It really brought home to me at that moment, that doing work for other people is its own reward.

A most memorable service was conducted, with great passion and verve as always. Now, in my life in the UK, I often think of this particular village and how my godchildren are getting on. We lost touch, and I worry whenever I hear typhoons, flooding or a volcanic eruption in the Philippines.

I will never forget my time in the Philippines. Six weeks: an amazing opportunity to listen, observe and learn the many pearls of wisdom that we in the West have lost or are gradually losing. There is no doubt in my mind that this experience as a kind of missionary defined my future path and made me want to support more communities that struggle and need support. I departed the Philippines humbled, and – hopefully – a kinder person, lessons learnt from the villagers I had spent time with. I left with a heavy heart, keen to stay longer, though I had envisaged this only as a stop off. I had a job in Hong Kong to get to. Life has a way of pressing you on.

One minute in the serenity and peace of the Philippine countryside, the next in the hustle and bustle of Gothic, tropical Hong Kong. I quickly adjusted – after all, I was not born to the Philippine way of life – but sometimes regretted the change. My life would be so different now if I had decided to stay, like John, in a rural environment like the Philippines. The conclusion I came to was that I had been spoiled by the ways of the West: materialism, travel, and an addiction to striving and achieving, competing, improving, doing better, feeling neverending guilt, self-hatred and jealousy of others! Do we need all this *stuff* we lust after? And why, when we succumb to possessions and endless bouts of retail therapy, are we never satisfied, always wanting more?

I believe we adjust to our environments as we find them. The people I met in the Philippine Highlands seemed more than content with their lives. To me, they seemed happy with their lot – I could not imagine them adjusting to a new life anywhere else. I'd liken my direct observations with the recorded experiences of the families of Gurkha soldiers, who were given the right to settle in the UK after a protracted legal battle. After a couple of years living in grey garrison towns, they reported that they longed for home; for the towns and villages where they were not foreigners, had their own independence and professions, and were respected to a much higher level.

John died in 2015 whilst visiting his brother back in the UK. My great friend Tim, John's nephew, went to the funeral in the Philippines and was astonished to see the extent of John's good work from over forty years in this country. Thousands of people turned up to attend the funeral service. Their huge grief is proof that he made a meaningful difference to many people's lives. I am a great believer in prayer when combined with positive action. I am of the belief that Jesus was a practical man, and that a true Christian should aim to do concrete good for people in the world. John was one of those rare, truly religious men who did. He practised in his life what he preached, and he was always loving and patient to the ordinary people he met – those who needed love and patience most.

I value practical Christianity, like John's, but practical faith comes in many forms, not just religious. The subconscious mind is an amazing thing. If we repeat affirmations on a regular basis, just as the Christians in the Philippines practised their Christian philosophy of love both to themselves and to their guests, then we – and others – start to show up as we *affirm* them to be. That, I think, is what struck me as so happy about the way of life in those villages, and why I found the people so full of wonder. In fact, the power of focused visualisation (faith!) can be almost frightening.

Let me give you an example. When I was in Palm Beach, Florida I wanted to go to Hong Kong. At that point, I did not have a job there. I did not know anybody there. I was unsure if my qualifications would allow me to work there. I just had this obsession with going to work in Hong Kong. It seemed like the most glamourous place in the world – I even plastered the walls of my flat with pictures of the place! And my unwavering focus, refusing to give up when I was rejected for job after job, eventually landed me with a job at Raffles. What we visualise *can* come true, if we refuse to let negative patterns of thinking and fear of failure stop us. If you fail, *learn* to see it as a setback rather than taking it a sign that you — *you yourself* — are personally wrong in your aspirations. *Have faith*. If I could transfer the same practical faith and belief that these amazing people in the Philippines had into my life and business, just think of the potential!

With faith, the effort to believe in yourself, and positive affirmations, your plans and dreams come to life. My only word of caution is: be careful what you dream for. Make sure it is worth it, and be precise about what you want and when you want it. For example, a system I now use for all my projects, events, objectives and goals is to map them out, imagine what the event will look like from every perspective, picture the teams of people taking part (including the crowds of cheering supporters), and visualise how the charities and sponsors will fit in. I then walk the initial route myself, to plan out where the main water stops, main checkpoints, and all the special effects and 'Wow' factor items will be. Then I sleep on it. While you are sleeping the mind gets to work putting it all together, and you wake refreshed, ready to enact your plan. Sleep is an extraordinary thing. Over twenty scientific studies all report the same findings. The shorter you sleep, the shorter your life. Adults over 45 years of age who sleep less than six hours a night are two hundred per cent more likely to have a heart attack or stroke in their lifetimes than those who sleep seven or eight hours a night. We are only just realising the full power of the subconscious mind for solving problems as we sleep, so this alone is a great reason to go to bed early, so sleep on it.

Practicality is important to me in my spirituality and my self-belief. Don't let yourself be caught up in *what might happen* or why you, as the world's worst failure, will never be able to get your idea off the ground. *Put your faith into practice*: be realistic, accept yourself and love yourself – and get on and do it!

POINTS FOR REFLECTION

- Learn, try and practise a wide range of skills, jobs and vocations.

- Stand out from the maddening crowd, be different and don't always follow sheep.

- Be active and get stuck in. Do the thing and you will have power.

- Become indispensable and always go the extra mile.

- Ensure you can fit your plan onto one A4 sheet of paper. Keep it simple.

- You can discover more about a person in an hour of play than in a year of conversation.

- Learn a new skill every year and become an expert in that skill.

- We cannot do great things we can only do little things with great love.

- Control your thoughts to bring about only desirable conditions.

- Every time we say 'I must do something' it takes an incredible amount of energy, far more than physically doing it.

- Worry a little bit every day and in a lifetime you will lose a couple of years. If something is wrong, fix it if you can, but train yourself not to worry. Worry never fixes anything.

- Do not procrastinate.

CHAPTER 4
PLANNING – CARSTENSZ PYRAMID

Planning: not avoiding risk, but choosing it.

Take your time to plan. Don't go rushing about willy-nilly: you need to make sure you are prepared. I learned this lesson the hard way when my friends and I attempted to climb the Carstenz Pyramid in West Papua, formerly Irian Jaya.

Christmas, 1998. Sitting by a roaring fireside in Kindrochit full of food, comfort and Christmas cheer, I was discussing my hopes for the future with one of my closest friends. As we gazed into the flames, I confessed my plans to Neil: in the New Year, I was going to leave my job and devote myself full-time to organising Challenge events – a risk, but one I had to take if I wanted to fulfil my Wild-Fox dreams. 'Brilliant!' Neil exclaimed. 'I have a suggestion for you. Why don't you begin your new journey with an adventure?' Neil had been planning to invite me on part of the 'Seven Summits' challenge he was undertaking, to climb the Carstensz Pyramid. An adventurer and explorer, Neil Laughton, who was also in the SAS territorials, had completed numerous challenges on land and sea, from Mauritius to Mount Everest. His latest mission was to climb the highest mountain on each of the seven continents, including Everest, Kilimanjaro and, now in Australasia, the Carstensz Pyramid: the highest summit between the Himalayas and the Andes. It is the most elusive of all the 'Seven Summits'. Gauntlet laid down, I accepted the challenge. A new challenge for the new millennium. I was ready for it.

Six weeks later we were flying to Bali. The team had spent a few sessions learning how to climb, abseil and belay in a converted church in Leith. Apparently this climb was a VS9, which meant very little to me. 'What's VS9?' I asked Neil. 'Very Severe Nine.'

He wasn't joking. I remember the reaction of a climbing instructor we were training with on Ben Nevis. When he found out what we were preparing to do, his shocked response was a stark reminder of the reality of our task: 'You will need months of intensive training to be able to manage these grades! We don't have *any* courses that would prepare you at such short notice!'

The Carstensz Pyramid resembles the spiky, ridged back of a monstrous lizard, rising from the misty foothills of the western highlands of Papua Province. At 4,884 metres high, it's the highest island peak in the world – and certainly looks like one of the most dramatic mountains on Earth. Its Indonesian name, Puncak Jaya, translates as 'Glorious Mountain', though it is still known as the Carstensz Pyramid among mountaineers. It is one of the remotest and most technically demanding of the Seven Summits, requiring a five-day hike through thick jungle before reaching base camp. There is no helicopter access from base camp, meaning that anyone injured during the climb can only return on foot. As well as this, the climb is widely known to be one of the wettest, slipperiest and most miserable of the seven ascents.

Having recently passed SAS selection (territorials), I was at the peak of my fitness: confident and foolhardy. I was excited! Another amazing adventure! I had visited Bali from Hong Kong when I was working there in the late 1980s, and I had always wanted to travel more in this part of the world. Deciding to commit to this trip was also the catalyst for leaving my job as director of a mobile phone communications company, in order to build up the Caledonian Challenge – the first large adventure challenge I was developing with my friend Angus MacDonald.

It was to be an extraordinary couple of weeks, with a few *too* many near death experiences for comfort. We had a couple of training weekends together in Scotland, but due to a combination of unforeseen issues and some lack of communication, two members of our team, Sean and Chris only joined at the last minute. Anyway, we were all experienced adventurers and quickly became fast friends. Arriving from Heathrow all together, we checked into our guesthouse on Kuta Beach, Bali, and headed straight for the beach.

The Pyramid itself can only be reached by local flight to a tiny village in the foothills, so we'd opted to stay the first few nights in Bali to train in the rainforest there. First, however, after the long flight, we were ready for a dip! Rugby ball and swimming trunks in hands, we trotted down to the famous surfing beaches of Bali. It took about twenty minutes of gentle training on the sand before anyone noticed that Neil was missing. I had clocked that he'd headed in for a swim, had not given it a second thought as Sean and I tossed the rugby ball to and fro. In those short minutes, Neil had been caught by a strong undertow and was engaged in a desperate struggle for his life! It was futile to fight the fierce current, and I do believe anyone but Neil would have drowned. With all his considerable strength he fought against the waves, using every ounce of his energy, and *just* managed to claw his way back. Back on the beach after half an hour, we saw Neil silently emerge from the water and sit down at the edge of the sea, staring out in contemplation, before he turned to us, clearing his throat, and revealed the dangerous extent of his brief battle for survival. We later discovered that in our instinctive dash for the beach, we had chosen to swim on a notoriously dangerous stretch of water. It was only in hindsight that I remembered seeing warning signs about dangerous currents. We had been planning for our climb and not for the unexpected – always expect the unexpected and remember that old Army adage: without prior planning and preparation, expect piss poor performance.

The unexpected can always catch us out, no matter how much we think we have prepared for every conceivable risk. Thinking of it afterwards, I could not remember other people swimming on that stretch of beach, but it was late in the afternoon – the sun was heading for bed – we had assumed that main beach-going hours were over. We headed for our accommodation, changed in silence, and went out to eat more sombre than before. Was this an ominous sign of other unpleasant things we had forgotten to take account of?

The plan was to head further into Bali and put in some practice climbing of one of the main volcanoes (inactive, I may add – we had checked up on that, at least). On impulse we hired four scooters, only to learn that Sean – a last-minute addition to our team – had never ridden one before. All we could do was give him a quick course in scooter skills before setting off to the mountain. 'Crash' course it certainly was: almost immediately Sean shot off out of control, taking out a honeymooning couple who were quietly pootling along on a Vespa. We retrieved Sean from the entanglement – it was pure luck that he, and indeed the poor couple, got away with just minor scratches and a few dents to vehicles and heads. We had been in Bali for no more than six hours and already ratcheted up several near-death experiences due to lack of preparation... it did not bode well. There is a balance here – over-planning and over-worrying means that many a project simply never gets off the starting block, and even if the rocket fuel has been enough and the jumbo jet takes off, the best made plans can and do go wrong all the time. Sometimes planning helps and sometimes no amount of planning or risk assessment will anticipate a catalogue of disasters. You need to be *ready* for anything, and in life, this simply is not possible. You need to be ready to be ready for anything, and there are times when to be 'can do' you are venturing into the unknown and surviving on a wing and a prayer. Planning is important, and yet so is having the confidence to have a go despite all the potential pitfalls, known and unknown, and make it work. This was one of those times.

The following morning we headed off into the interior of the island for our first day of proper local training. After three hours of blissfully uneventful riding we chose a mountain, left the bikes with a friendly looking villager (they'd be fine! They'd probably be fine...) and set off up the first obvious path we could see. We soon realised what anyone in Bali could have informed us if we'd bothered to do any research: locals are not interested in climbing hills, so mountain paths peter out very quickly. This dawned on us when we realised we were hacking through primary jungle-type terrain. I remember thinking grimly of my SAS training, and how useful a machete would have been at this point. The company and adrenaline kept spirits high, though. Another fantastic adventure and we were still making good headway in these humid, clammy conditions.

As the hours passed, Summit Fever gripped the gang. It was growing dark: in the tropics, night came at around 5.50pm. Should we risk trying for the summit in darkness, or turn around? Take the risk and crack on through the unknown, of course! It was then that the rain started in earnest, as an almighty monsoon storm hit the region. Alright, this was a sign from the heavens: this was our cue to start heading back – and what a descent it was. Sliding, running, slipping, desperately clutching on to vines, bark, or anything that would slow our descent. At one point in the madness I almost laughed out loud, when the bizarre image came into my mind that it was as though we were sliding down the back of a greasy, mud-bathing dragon. We made it back to the bikes (deserted by their guardians – but miraculously still there) in the pitch dark. We were soaked, scratched, and bleeding through the caked-in mud. What an introduction to Bali.

The day ended with Sean getting a puncture. Of course, we had no puncture repair kit... after only a couple of hours of negotiating we managed to flag down a truck to take him back to town while the rest of us biked back.

We were now as ready as we'd ever be for the main adventure, and flew to the region of Irian Jaya (now West Papua province) via the Spice Islands. We were mindful of the fact that we were the first major expedition to attempt the Carstensz Pyramid since a group of mountaineering students from Cambridge University were captured by local Dani tribes. Two of the team were stabbed to death and there were several other fatalities in the skirmish before the group was rescued by Indonesian special forces. Tribespeople were protesting against the invasive creation of a huge goldmine that the Indonesian Government was building in the area, apparently causing massive soil erosion and deforestation. However reasonable, their protest was still of concern to us. Then, during our night's stopover in the Spice Islands, I politely accepted a drink when we arrived at our guesthouse... and succumbed to the dreaded Delhi Belly. Not the best time to fall ill, and easily preventable – I would be in need of every ounce of energy for the huge challenge ahead. Lessons learnt: always drink sealed bottled water, fizzy drinks or boiled water – for instance, tea.

We arrived in Irian Jaya and then moved to the goldmine itself, where we met up with an Indonesian team who had climbed Everest the previous year, and also a team of 'compassus'. These Indonesian armed guards were necessary in the tense local political climate. They carried ancient rifles and did not have boots – they looked thoroughly miserable to be with us. To add to the fun, the region was experiencing some of its worst weather for years, with torrential rain, sleet and snow further up the mountain. Used to Scotland, I joked that I felt very much at home, but this was alien weather for the locals.

We began our climb the next day at a steady pace, alongside our entourage of armed guards and a couple of porters. However, after a first night in freezing conditions, we woke to find our entourage had upped sticks and buggered off back down the mountain! The unfortunate Sean was left to discover that he had unwisely put his sleeping bag in with the main camp kit, and the porters had taken it with them. To be honest, I'd already decided that the guards would have been useless in the face of attack, and had been planning ways of extracting their weapons should this happen... however, in this case my ingenious fulminations were unnecessary; it was an uneventful trek to base camp.

We were set on making the summit now, even though the weather was clearly not right for the attempt and our supplies were quickly running out since the support team had vanished. Another example in hindsight of a badly-thought-out decision and an example of how things can go wrong on a mountain expedition. We couldn't have planned for the magical disappearing support team, but all mountaineers should make allowance for variations in weather. We had not anticipated these extreme conditions, and should have turned back at this point. However, the overwhelming desire to achieve a summit doesn't often take basic common-sense into account; factor in the pressure from sponsors, the huge costs of expeditions such as these, the loss of face in turning back, not to mention the egos and pride involved... still, lack of preparation is a recipe for disaster.

On Summit Day we debated but decided to carry on heading up and soon came face to face with a massive, sheer rock face, covered in snow and ice. Due to unforeseen levels of cloud coverage, we could only guess at the size of the entire face, clouds swirling around the rocks, clearing for seconds before returning. Neil led the way, followed by the Indonesian team, then me, Chris and Sean at the back. Then with no warning at all, a spatter of gravel fell on my head, followed by an ominous rumble... a couple of boulders had been worked loose by Neil, and I heard a warning shout: 'Keep your heads into the face! Don't look up!' The tumbling boulders barely missed us by inches – in fact, one caught Sean directly on his rucksack, making him overbalance and almost tipping him off the cliff. Had he slipped then, we would have probably held his weight, as we were all roped together – but I'd not like to have found out. Several more rock alarms, including a few even closer misses, resulted in some angry exchanges, particularly from those of us lower down on the face. Still, we were creeping on up, despite being unable to plan more than a foot or so ahead.

Climbing is always a lottery. No matter the level of skill or amount of experience, you can never prepare for the unexpected. The sudden collapse of an ice shelf, the crumbling away of a hold that felt firm at first test, loose footings, sliding surfaces, your path over a glacier simply melting away; the list is endless. And we were all relatively unskilled, inexperienced amateurs – Neil and the two Indonesians the only ones of us with much experience.

We then came to a seriously large overhang, which forced a bottleneck among us. How on earth were we supposed to climb over this? Hanging off the edge, we did our best to discuss reasonable options and decided to struggle around it, finally making it to the top ridge a mere four hours later. It was clear that, in order to reach the summit, we had to stop and make fresh plans. Something had to give. Swallowing my momentary chagrin, I accepted that it was for the best that Neil and the Indonesians continue alone to one of the many ridge Pinnacles in order to qualify for an official 'bagging' of the mountain.

Now, I may not have reached this technical milestone, but that doesn't mean I didn't summit the Carstensz Pyramid, any less than Neil and our teammates. I'm genuinely proud to have made the decision to wait behind them so that they could carry on. Expeditions like this one are made as a team effort: if part of the team is successful, the whole team is. Even if we had made mistakes along the way, the important thing was that Neil, Sean, Chris and I had trained, had a laugh, kept each other cheerful, and kept each other going through tough times – from start to finish, we worked *together*.

When Neil and the Indonesians returned, we commenced our cautious descent off the mountain. Usually, more accidents happen on the way down a mountain such as this than on the ascent, so we took our time and were back at base camp later in the afternoon. We'd done it! We'd achieved the objective of our trip, and we were then lucky enough to spend some time with the Dani tribe in the inner regions of Irian Jaya. Michael Rockefeller, of the famous American millionaire dynasty, had been sailing past this area in the 1960s on a quest for Guinean art, and disappeared. It later transpired that parts of his body were ceremonially eaten by a local tribe... to this day they reportedly still practice a form of cannibalism. It is apparently common for enemy tribes to eat their foe after a skirmish (saving the heads, which are shrunken in order to gain the enemy's strength) and I couldn't help wondering if our bodies were being eyed up for the pot. Any time someone came up behind me in that village, I jumped a mile! Were they looking at us, thinking 'lunch?'

We returned to Bali the following week for a couple of days of much-needed R&R. Our troubles were over, and it seemed to be clear sailing from here on in... the trouble is, when sailing, storms blow up fast.

We had all received a severe battering on the mountain with endless cuts and bruises – I was particularly suffering, with amoebic dysentery still raging through my intestines. Arriving back in Bali, we headed off to the beach for the second time for a final swim (taking particular care to ensure we chose our swimming spot more wisely, this time). Returning to our rooms refreshed, we began getting ready for our last night on the town, when Neil suddenly announced that he felt terrible and couldn't go on. His arm was badly hurting – one of his cuts seemed to have become infected after the swim. We left him resting, and went to the Sari

Night club (so sadly bombed a few years later) but none of us could keep our minds on clubbing, and soon returned to the hotel to keep Neil company. As our last night went by, Neil's state deteriorated, his arm swelling to huge proportions overnight. We boarded the aircraft swiftly the next day, wanting to get back to Blighty with minimal incident. Neil, in agony, was taken straight to hospital on landing. He had septicemia and ended up staying in hospital for a week before he was released.

Overall, it was a trip that will be remembered for its great perils and challenges. When I think of the ease with which our lives could have been taken at whim! A rock moving an inch to the right, a foot slipping and dragging our human chain off the mountain, any one of Sean's accidents, a thousand times any of us could have poisoned ourselves, drowned, or neglected a scratch. Could we have avoided these dangers in the first place? Sometimes, yes. Writing my book now, I can point to these idiotic mistakes, hope that others can learn from them and laugh. *Will* humans ever learn from others, or do we only learn through our own stupidity? The worst experiences teach the best lessons, or so they say... there is real food for thought here.

I'm fascinated by the human desire to push oneself through impossible tasks in order to hazard a chance at success. Summit Fever is the perfect example of this. Who would have cared, apart from the climbers, if we had given up in unsafe conditions? *Was* it just pride that carried us on up; and the fear of 'losing face'? The truth is that no-one really gives a damn about what you do. A couple of empathetic family members, a few friends if you're lucky – but ultimately, what matters in life is what gives *you* a sense of self-worth.

In this chapter, I've emphasised our lack of preparation and the easily avoidable ways we made life difficult for ourselves during this trip. I became ill because I broke the cardinal rule of not drinking anything unless it had been boiled or was presented in a sealed bottle. So I got amoebic dysentery, making for a thoroughly miserable ascent of a perilous mountain requiring possession of all one's wits. The most major risk we took, however, was undertaking to climb the Cartensz Pyramid in the first place. The message I want to demonstrate in this chapter is *not* to avoid risk, at all costs! It is that, in life, we need to plan *risk* against *return*. We shouldn't be cavalier with ourselves and others (always, always check for currents when swimming in unknown waters). Instead, take *planned risks* and gain those heartstopping moments that, in your life, stand above and beyond the everyday.

We think we are invincible when in fact we are incredibly vulnerable. Only one month ago, I was clearing bush off the shore of Loch Tay, as farmers have done for centuries. My finger was accidentally spiked by a blackthorn, which led to serious septicemia just like Neil's. Four weeks and two courses of antibiotics later, the inflammation is still there and will not leave. Before the age of antibiotics, I could have died. As we grow older we hopefully build up an increased sense of risk-ver-sus-return, but any little thing could still get us, in the end. Think of Lawrence of Arabia dying of a motorbike crash after all his adventures in the Mid-dle East – there is so much danger in the world. Equally, however, a life wrapped in cotton wool is no life at all. In business, love, or daily life, risk is unavoidable. After all, pushing boundaries, chal-lenging oneself, setting records, and having fun is what living life to the full is all about! When we look back on our lives, it is the moments of terror, adrenaline, relief, and times of true friendship like the Carstensz Pyramid expedition that we remem-ber with great fondness. I would not exchange these moments for the world.

POINTS FOR REFLECTION

- Establish your own personal space – it must be sound-proof – where you can focus on the mission, the plan, the project. Seek silence frequently.

- Learn to keep the door shut, keep out of your mind and get out of your world every element that seeks admittance with no definite helpful end in view.

- Go where you can be alone to concentrate your thoughts on your one innermost sincere desire, where you can impress that desire upon your subconscious mind without distraction.

- Draw large colourful mind-maps (both short and long term) with as much detail and as many photographs, drawings and diagrams as possible. Use A2 paper and good quality colour pens. Hang the mind maps up where you can see them every day. Adjust, alter and update the plans as the flashes of inspiration arrive.

- Record your detailed plans and objectives on a voice recorder. Refine and update them as you listen to them first thing in the morning and last thing at night.

- Strongly believe and mentally picture that you are actually living your project. Visualise that you are in possession of your goal/plan. Think through the many challenges and problems concerning your plan. Sleep on it and later the mind will provide the answers and directions via revelations from the subconscious mind.

- Think of three things that make you roar with laughter and store these images.

- Think of three situations where your mind is at complete ease, totally relaxed. This will put you onto a higher plane of inspiration and creativity. Find your creative zone - you will discover it when you are on your higher plane

- We become what we think about so plan what you want to become.

- 95% of our time seems to be focused on the problems and only 5% on finding solutions. We must use time creatively in the knowledge that the time is always right to do right.

- The only sure way to avoid making mistakes is to have no new ideas.

- Joy in looking and comprehending is nature's most beautiful gift.

- To change the effect you must change the cause.

- The possibilities of thought training are infinite. Its consequences are eternal and yet few take the pains to direct their thinking into channels that will do them good, but instead leave all to chance.

CHAPTER 5
POSITIVEROSITY – KINDROCHIT, SAS SELECTION AND THE BIRTH OF WILDFOX EVENTS

POSITIVEROSITY: A law of attraction.
Be positive, drive your own destiny, and you
will overcome all your obstacles..

With everything prepared, you just need an injection of momentum. This is where positiverosity comes into play! When I first had the idea for Wild-Fox Events, I knew this challenge wouldn't be easy. Passing SAS selection gave me the ability to always think positively: this is essential in manifesting your dreams into reality.

Just before the turn of the millennium, when I was 35 years old, two things happened that solidified the course of my life. Until then I had been travelling the world, adventuring and working in hospitality and catering, but now I was ready to put some bigger dreams into action, using the self-knowledge and life lessons my previous escapades had taught me.

It all started with Kindrochit. Having travelled the world, I had begun to find myself dreaming of a place to call home. As a creature of nature, I couldn't see myself as a city-dweller. I sought somewhere remote, amongst the majestic natural landscape of Scotland, somewhere to inspire creation, freedom of thought and adventure; a base from which I could continue on my journey, a firm foundation. I found all that and more in Kindrochit.

Situated on the banks of Loch Tay in Perthshire, miles from anything, the house has a truly magical quality. You can breathe the rich air of the Highlands, stare all day at Ben Lawers over the majestic loch, and climb mountains from your own front door. An opportunity came up to rent Kindrochit, a farmhouse owned by my sister and brother-in-law. I will always be grateful that they gave me the chance to move there, and from the moment I first saw it, I knew this was the place I'd been dreaming of.

As with everything worth having, though, there were obstacles. The house had no heating (a serious drawback in the biting Highland winters), no furniture, and was run-down from years of neglect. Far from being put off by these facts, they endeared the house even further to me. I saw it as a project, something to pour my energies into. I loved the house for its character and stunning view, and wasn't about to give it up over a lack of a few home comforts – I'd been in far worse situations, after all! But, I needed a plan. I had no savings, and nothing but a borrowed second-hand car, a basic Belling cooker with three electric rings, an ancient, wood-fired Rayburn oven which took days to heat the house's rooms up, a log fire in the sitting room, and some mice for companions. I had to think of something to bring in some income, and also inspire me. The remote location was the biggest problem I faced in finding a suitable way to make money, as, beautifully stunning as it was, it had zero job prospects unless I fancied becoming a shepherd. I didn't know it then, but I was on my way to discovering the second thing that would transform my life and give me an ultimate purpose.

My first July at Kindrochit, my friend Angus MacDonald asked me to join him and a group of fellow endurance enthusiasts in undertaking an ambitious challenge: 32 Munros (a mountain over 3000ft) in four days. It was a crazy challenge, but, determined, we set out to accomplish it. As it happened, I was the last man standing, the only one to complete the full 32 Munros. I nearly didn't make it – I had to flee down Stob Binnein when it was hit by a violent thunderstorm. My great aunt Janet had actually lost her life in curiously similar circumstances, after being struck by lightning on that very mountain. As I rushed to escape the wind and rain I imagined her ghost, who is said to be seen wearing her kilt, with her long, red hair flowing out behind her. She was only 24. I thought of this storm as a message from her: a sign telling me to go out and achieve something great, something she might have done, had her life not been cut so tragically short. Having made it down the mountain and completed the challenge, I was happy to have been the only one to do it. However, I was even happier to have had an idea of how to turn my passion into an income: somewhere along the way, during those four days, inspiration had struck me. When I set out, I had no idea I was beginning the inaugural Caledonian Challenge, and embarking on the adventure that would become WildFox Events.

What if this could be turned into something *big*, an endurance event in support of charitable causes? Angus and I discussed the concept and I knew it was my purpose. I couldn't stop thinking about it, growing more and more excited and inspired the more I did. Gradually, step by step, a plan was formed. As a mass event, this Munro concept was just not going to work, so a strategy was devised to move the event onto the famous West

Highland Way (a renowned drovers' road stretching from Glasgow all the way to Fort William, which was later improved by the military road systems of Generals Wade and Caulfield). I had taken part in a similar event, the MacLehose Trailwalker event in Hong Kong, in 1995. Along with 4000 other keen participants, I walked 100 kilometres in 24 hours, in support of Oxfam. It was a wonderful experience – the question was, would something like it work on the West Coast of Scotland, nearly three hours from any major city? I had no way of knowing, so I thought, well, why not give it a go? Twenty years later, this one single idea has led to a business that's created over 18 major events encouraging people to get out and challenge themselves in the country-side, while also raising amounts to the tune of well over £40 million pounds for charity. This does not include all the thousands raised by participants for their own chosen charitable causes over and above the event-nominated causes.

I didn't know that at the time, though. I had an idea – but how was I going to go about putting it into practice? It would never have been possible without the concept of positiverosity. Positiverosity involves having faith in one's own abilities, the eradication of procrastination and excuses, and a total blanking out of the fear and doubt that hold countless people back from ever even attempting to achieve their dream in the first place. I have come to realise it is an essential element to getting any project off the ground. Positiverosity means, above all else, 'feeling the fear' and 'doing it anyway'!

A major obstacle to positiverosity is insecurity. What happens if I have no income for several weeks or months? Can I get a loan or family support? What if no-one signs up? What if someone dies on the event? Overcoming these doubts involves resolve, resilience, determination, faith and confidence. Positiverosity also requires complete commitment. Many people draw back from taking the chances necessary to achieve their dream, or are simply unable to risk having no food on the table, no funds for the mortgage, no petrol for the car, no way to pay off the credit card bill – the list goes on and on. So, they settle for the secure, steady option of working for someone else, abandoning their dream and living a life without passion. Remember: if it were easy, everyone would be living their dream. But is it worth the risk? Absolutely! I had to learn to tighten the belt, or screw the nut as they say in the parachute regiment, and clamp down on all unnecessary outgoings and expenses. I bought a sack of tatties and lived on it for two weeks – only add cheese when you've overcome and obstacle and made some small success! Pasta and ragù was another favourite of mine from this time – it's easy to make and you never get bored of it. Every penny saved is a step on the way to achieving your dreams.

I had no qualifications in the outdoors and event organising roles apart from various experiences working in hotels and catering, and no savings – when you work for someone else, you are always paid just enough to survive, but never enough to set up on your own. I knew that I also lacked the toughness and fitness to take on the immense physical challenge of organising this 24-hour event. I would have to complete the event myself first, and would also need to present the challenge with authority to companies and groups up and down the country. This seemed a daunting task. The only thing that gave me confidence was the fact that out of the original sixteen that set out with Angus MacDonald and I that day in July, I was the only one to complete all 32 Munros. If I could do that, I could do this new challenge. Couldn't I? Hmm – maybe I needed a short, sharp shock, some new way of toughening myself up. I needed to test myself to the limits, beyond any limit I'd been to before, to build in a further layer of resilience, stubbornness, grit, determination, steel and fortitude. But how? This had to be something bigger than I could achieve on my own, something that would give me the authority and know-how to make my company a huge success. Then it hit me: I had unfinished business holding me back and affecting my confidence. I would try one more time to prove myself mentally and physically tough enough to pass SAS selection.

SAS selection is one of the most difficult military training programs in the world. Its purpose is to test candidates to the utmost limit of their physical and mental abilities. Though rare, it is not unheard of for candidates to die during the selection process. As with any elite fitness training and the pursuit of excellence, the unexpected can happen. I had witnessed a man drown when I did a stint in the Parachute Regiment TA. I knew the risks. It is not a game. I had attempted selection once before, eight years previously, and had passed all the major weekends, battlecamp and continuation, only to be failed on a weapons recognition test at the eleventh hour. I had never forgiven myself for coming so close only to fall at the final hurdle, and I had to settle this unfinished business before I reached the age limit. I was doing it for much more than that, however.

I had a motive for the madness. While the process would require a huge amount of commitment, time and resources, as a bonus I would be paid by Her Majesty, and this training would complement my plans. I would continue to serve in the TA unit part time whilst I built up the Caledonian Challenge.

So, I drove down to the squadron centre near Dundee and signed up for course 54, winter selection. Step one: commitment. Check. Now I just needed to get fit enough to actually be able to complete the course... I set myself a rigorous training schedule – circuit training, a heart-thumping ten-mile circuit over four Corbets (hills over 2000ft high – two-thirds as high as a Munro), canoeing, running circuits, press-ups, sit-ups – with tougher routes and longer distances as I progressed. It was hell, but I figured the more I put myself through at this stage, the easier I would find the weekends and, ultimately, the test week in the Brecon Beacons in Wales.

The winter selection course consisted of ten weekends over six months spent in a variety of remote training areas in Wales, at the other end of the country, including training every Wednesday evening. A huge commitment, especially for those who had full-time jobs, family, or other responsibilities. I already knew the winter selection was going to be tougher than the summer course I'd done in the nineties (Adam Ballinger has written an account of this in his book *The Quiet Soldier: On Selection with 21 SAS*, in which I feature as 'Folkes' – many reprints later, it has become a must-read for those thinking of attempting selection). On that course I was at my supreme fittest, and came either first or second on every weekend challenge. This was going to be very different – I was 35 years old, well past my prime, and not as fit as I was during my first attempt. It was also a 400-mile, 8-hour drive from Aberfeldy to the Brecon Beacons, so my fellow Scottish recruits and I spent endless hours cramped in the back of a rumbling V8 Land Rover driving there, to Elan Valley or the Black Mountains. Every Friday we would check into the Dundee squadron after a long week's work, where we'd prep kit and start driving by 10pm. We would arrive around nine hours later in the middle of the Brecons and then be launched straight into an exhausting two-day exercise before rumbling another nine hours back up the road to jock land. We were at a huge disadvantage! The squadrons in the south turned up at the location well before midnight, and got six hours of peaceful kip before the main exercise began. (It would have made sense to have created a Scotland-based selection course, which would have attracted many more potential recruits, but everything comes down to cost-effectiveness, and in the end one course for all squadrons is more economical than two. Like every public or civil service operation, costs are all that matter and little thought goes into the actual effect on the poor recruits. The Army and NHS are no different, with the endless cuts imposed upon them every year. God help us if we have another major conflict with an ever-diminishing defence force.) The Welsh recruits were even luckier, with a mere 40-minute drive to the location. Very unfair, and a major reason the jocks lost many excellent recruits – they simply couldn't handle the long hours spent travelling. Selection on its own is more than hard enough, but when you add in a hectic full-time work week, a massive commute to the South and the sleep deprivation that entails, mixed with your standard miserable British weather and depressing, dull, damp and dreary winter days, you create a recipe for a much bigger challenge than you originally imagined.

But, life is like that! You build resilience and toughness so that when the shit hits the fan and the world feels like it's against you, you have the ability to stick with your goals and see them through. Outdoor events – and life! – can throw anything at you. You need a level head and resolve of steel to keep going. For my part, I knew that the responsibility of having 1600 people walking 54 miles in 24 hours through the Scottish Highlands with the constant threat of driving lashing rain, and the pitch black, takes a certain amount of character. What if something were to go wrong? The buck would stop with me – no ifs, ands or buts! I knew I had to prepare for it, both physically and mentally, and every second I endured of the SAS selection procedure and the conditions we travelled in to get there would all help develop my character and resilience to tackle the long-term plan and the bigger picture.

As the weeks and months went by, the selection weekends became increasingly tougher, with more weights in the bergans (rucksacks), longer distances, and more challenging routes. One of the most challenging was the weekend spent in Elan Valley, which is totally featureless with no obvious reference points by which to navigate. The whole landscape is taken up with thousands of tufts of horrible, boggy, marshy terrain known in the regiment rather morbidly as 'babies' heads'. After six weeks, the entire Scottish recruit team that had started out was reduced to just two miserable victims: myself, and a tough jock who looked like Rumplestiltskin and had a fiery temper. What a contrast to my selection eight years earlier with 21 SAS! Then, there were 16 of us, with shorter trips to training and stunning summer weather, more atmosphere and a lot more espirit de corps. This time, with just my angry friend for companionship on the long journeys and tough weekends, the mental aspects of the course were much tougher. My experiences eight years ago now seemed like jolly rambles through lush terrain under the beaming sunshine: this time around the weekends consisted of lonely, silent slogs through impossible courses in the dark.

Soon, though, weekend nine was upon us: 'The High Walk'. A forced march up and over a mountain twice in a given time. Failure to meet the grade meant instant recourse, or binning, depending on how late your time was. Despite our exhaustion and the difficulty of the course, both Rumplestiltskin and I were able to pass! Our reward? Moving on to phase two, which consisted of a further nine weekends of continuation training (learning all the skills of the regiment), culminating in a tough two-week battlecamp where all your skills and training were put into practice. On the very last exercise, everyone was captured and put through a gruelling mock interrogation (this is known as 'resistance to interrogation training'), which was made pretty hellish and realistic, although nothing on par with the real thing. Finally, a full year after enrolling in the selection course, the coveted winged dagger beret was placed upon my head, and I joined 23 SAS regiment. In doing so, I had also buried a skeleton of my past, and completed unfinished business. I had never been so fit, and had been pushed to my absolute limits. I had contracted the flu in my final two-week battle camp, which had seriously affected my energy levels. In hindsight, and considering part of the battlecamp involved live fire, I was very lucky not to be recoursed or worse, but I had endured. I felt I had achieved the greatest physical challenge of my life, and the experience had changed me for the better.

Before I go any further, I want to get one thing straight. I'm not talking about my training in the special forces for any reason other than it so effectively highlights the strengths I've developed at least in part through that experience, strengths that have stood me in great stead ever since. I'm not a war hero, I've never been on active service as Her Majesty never called me up during my time, however the skills I learned through this training have taught me to remain calm under fire – real and theoretical – to remain positive and keep perspective under extreme stress. I would go so far as to say that these skills have saved my life on more than one occasion.

What are the traits I learned as an SAS soldier, and why are these traits so important to everyday life?

1   Humility is key! Be a team player.
2   An unrelenting pursuit of excellence.
3   Trust, honesty and commitment.
4   High levels of motivation and energy.
5   Fitness standards equivalent to Olympic athletes.
6   Cheerfulness in the face of adversity.
7   Never give up!
8   Self-reliance.

9 How to cope under extreme pressure.
10 Mental strength, and the ability to push through
    pain barriers.
11 Be able to switch your aggression on and off, like a tap.
12 The ability to question a plan.

We all possess different levels of these traits within us, but it is worth working hard to acquire the ones you may not already have to achieve full positiverosity. Most important is humility. No matter how good or special we think we are, we are all brought down to Earth sooner or later. We will not be young forever: the body weakens with age, and illness and injury creep up on us with ever-increasing vigour as our days pass. We are mere mortals, after all – even those who pass SAS selection. The only difference is an ability to dig deeper than the next man and build up an attitude of mental toughness far beyond what the untrained person is capable of.

All those traits, from humility, to self-reliance have been invaluable to me in setting up Wild-Fox and its events over the years. Without having learned these traits in selection, I doubt very much that I would have been able to see my dream through. The key is to remember that anything worth having is worth training for, and that these traits are well worth perfecting. Build up the belief that you can achieve your dream in the subconscious mind, rehearse it over and over again, visualise its intimate workings: believe things are going to transpire, and they will. The subconscious will take over and start to develop blueprints to help you achieve your goal. Trust me – it's worked every time for me, and it will for you. The key, once again, is positiverosity: remain in a highly positive frame of mind, believe in yourself, and the outcome *will* turn out as you have predicted.

The next part of positiverosity is dedication to the pursuit of excellence. You can't argue with someone who gives it their best, day after day after day. I learned that during selection: we spent hours and hours going through training manoeuvres, over and over again until they became second nature, automatic reactions. The more we practice, the better we become. The more we rehearse, the better we perform at the crucial moment, when any minor fault could mean failure. During parachute training, we spent the entire first week in the hangar, practicing landings over and over again, landing the correct way, forwards, backwards, in the dark, landing on buildings, into water. Dangerous situations like getting out of entanglements, air steal, and parachute malfunction were drilled again and again and again. It was only after seven days of endlessly repeating these motions, until we could do them without even thinking, that we were permitted to enter the Hercules C130 aircraft for the real thing...

Go! Go! Go! I shuffled to the tail of the C130 Hercules. The rear ramp was down and we were parachuting into the deep pearly waters of the Mediterranean Sea. I focused on my feet as I stumbled, trying to keep my balance as I inched slowly towards the plunge.

Go! I was off. As soon as I left the aircraft my feet were ripped from under me as I was sucked out of the back of the Hercules, followed by a rasp of silk and then the relaxing sensation of gliding down, down, down towards the enchanting, enticing deep blue sea. Minutes later the life jacket reacted as it made contact with the water and inflated tightly around my neck and chest, and there I was floating like a Michelin man. One minute I was in the heart of the noisy Hercules being hurled around in the turbulence, deafening engines groaning away, nervous faces all round, anxious glances, checking of equipment, life jackets, reserves, rifles and packs, and then after a thrilling exit and flight I was floating around in complete silence.

We were on a two-week exercise with the squadron and Cyprus was the destination. A full day on the ranges testing all the weapons, followed by a brutal ten-mile battle march in two hours in full battle dress with bergen and weapons in the searing Cyprus heat was followed by a spectacular joint exercise with the Royal Navy. It struck home how easy it is to get bumped off in conflict, there are so many opportunities to get cut down from every angle, especially when you are attacking a well fortified position. Think Gallipoli, just up the coast from where we were, think of all those past conflicts where our forefathers were mown down by endless machine gun batteries in World Wars One and Two. Wind the clock forward to today, and the weaponry is even more deadly, accurate and far-reaching. Add in all the night vision and heat detecting equipment and we really do not have much of a chance in modern warfare. Snipers can now be accurate at over two miles, terrifying when you have no chance of even seeing the enemy before they fire.

Thoughts of my paternal grandfather in action are never far from my mind in such circumstances. Billy Fox-Pitt fought in both world wars and headed up one of the first machine gun platoons as a founding member of the Welsh Guards 1915 during WWi at the battle of Loos. It is hard to imagine or contemplate what hellish conditions they must have endured. One of his diary notes mentioned having a 'good shoot' that day rather like describing a pheasant shoot in the country. What did he mean by a 'good shoot' and how many men had been taken out with this deadly new weapon? We now use the modern GPMG (general purpose machine gun) which has not advanced much from the machine guns used in WWI. Billy must have had nine lives plus, and he was wounded, repatriated back to the UK, recovered and was sent out again several times over the course of the war. Have humans learnt anything from the futility of war and will it happen again? The answer is simple: we have not learnt much, and it will happen again. We somehow think we are living in an enlightened new age where we are above the stupidity of our forebears. One hundred years on from WWI and what have we learnt? As memories dwindle and new generations forget the horrors of the past how can we prevent a major war from happening again?

Before long we were heading into a night exercise flying into central Cyprus. We were in sticks of four-man patrols and the objective was to land, tab a few miles and lie up observing enemy positions before joining the main group.

Night jumps were always strange as you could not see what you were jumping into. Just a black void, followed by a peaceful glide to earth and then panic as you anticipated hitting the ground, or indeed water, or anything for that matter. You just prayed that the pilot had chosen the landing site wisely. A few years earlier a stick of lads had been dropped in Portugal on a night exercise but the pilot had misjudged the height from the ground and many of the parachutes were only half open when they landed, resulting in some horrific injuries in-

cluding a broken back and broken legs. It was miracle no one had died but it left a nagging concern in
the back of your mind. Was our pilot experienced
or had he just joined the squadron? Was he familiar with the terrain and geography of the country?
How many flights had he taken before and importantly how many night jumps had he been responsible for?

Before a jump everyone is naturally appre-
hensive, focused, going through the actions in their
minds, actions on twists, air steals, entanglements
– equipment not dropping below when clips are released in flight normally resulting in a broken leg.
The weather is always a concern. The mind wanders
during these anxious moments of waiting – waiting
to be called up to the aircraft, waiting to load, waiting for the craft to take off, the innocuous diesel
fumes, the overbearing heat, sweat from carrying
all the kit, dehydration, nerves, waiting and waiting
and then before we know it we are rumbling down
the runway.

It's easy to imagine the parachute regiments
dropping in to enemy territory during operations in
WW2, Normandy landings, Arnhem, etc. They had
the added terror of knowing that all below would
be hostile and hell-bent on taking you out. During
the Normandy landings in 1944 many paratroopers
landed directly onto enemy positions, many were
shot before they even touched the ground, many

drowned in the flooded plains and many were caught up in trees and buildings and were eventually shot when discovered unless they were able to free themselves. Many of the aircraft were shot down before the poor chaps had a chance to leap out and some landed miles from their targets having become disorientated with all the enemy firing flak and explosions. I have been fortunate enough to meet some of veterans from D-Day when we organised a 44 mile walk along the Normandy beaches. It was a great honour to talk to them.

The command to stand by was given and our stick stood up, adjusted our equipment and jostled into position. I was the fourth to jump in my stick of four men. We began the frantic last-minute adjustments of equipment, helmet checks, parachute and reserve checks, kit check ensuring the clips were all primed and ready for release once out of the aircraft, using the buddy-buddy system where we check each other's kit and ensure our static line is correctly attached. The other sticks sat and watched as we prepped ourselves and pulled ourselves together for the jump. Focus, focus, remember to punch out of the aircraft as hard as possible into the 120mph slip stream, keep close to the chap in front for every delayed second in jumping equates to a couple of hundred yards gap on the ground. The side door opened in preparation as the violent wind rushed past, the noise of the C130 engines intensified to an ear-splitting whine and anxiety levels shot up. This is it, brace yourself, we are off!

The red light came on giving us a 10-second warning, followed by green and the first chap was gone. We all shuffled forward, keeping as close as possible. Go! Go! went numbers two and three, and then it was my turn. The plane was being buffeted about and it was tricky to keep a good balance. I lurched forward, tripped, head butted the poor RAF exit crew and we ended up in a heap on the floor. We recovered rapidly and I was expelled from the plane by the two RAF chaps rather like a Jack Russell being hurled over a fence. Out I went like a bag of washing and immediately became entangled, upside down in the parachute strings and webbing. In those precious seconds I fought with all my might, trying desperately to untangle myself and right my position. No sooner had I straightened out than I hit the ground with an almighty thump. A close run thing and it would have been a very different story had I landed head first.

Life periodically throws unexpected curved balls at us. What caused the sudden stumble? What would have happened had I not been able to extract myself from the twisted descent? Would I have ended up dead or in a wheelchair? We will never know. It is the same in life and business. We need to be alert to all possibilities but it is often the unexpected that will catch us out and we need to figure every possibility into the plan and prepare accordingly. On this occasion I was lucky.

Excellence only comes from practice – endless, repetitive practice. You must have the dedication, commitment and motivation to put in the work. Commitment only comes when you have the right frame of mind and that is where positiverosity plays such a vital role.

THE PRINCIPLES OF POSITIVEROSITY

Positive mental attitude, or positiverosity as I call it, goes hand in hand with the laws of attraction. Never underestimate how powerful being positive is. If you smile, people smile back at you. If you scowl you will receive a scowl in return. Try it.

Be positive in life and in turn you will attract positiverosity and powerful positive results will fall into place. Obstacles will melt away and a path will appear to help you proceed with your plans.

Get into the daily habit of being hugely grateful for what you *already* have, no matter how little you think that is. Gratitude transforms what we have into enough and more. Generate your own inner strength of gratitude and positive thought and you will radiate more energy to be positive to those you meet.

Re-affirm your belief and faith thoughts. Believe you will achieve your dreams and re-affirm this every day. Train the subconscious mind to accept this as normal. Believe in your goal, feel it and visualise it becoming a reality. Catch your mind's inner chatter every time it has a negative thought. Re-affirm only positive thoughts. Become an expert in cultivating your creative thought processes. This will take weeks and months of awareness and eventually you will dispel negative chatter.

Never hold a grudge or animosity towards anybody as it will affect your ability to retain positive energy levels. Don't dwell on it. Let go of criticism and move on.

Learn not to worry about things that you have no power to change. Worrying is destructive thought. Emit a new signal with your thoughts and feelings and you will regain the power of your creative self.

Take the Artemis Great Kindrochit Quadrathlon, for example. When I first dreamed up this event, which starts on the Ardtalnaig shore of Loch Tay near my home, Kindrochit, for a 1.35km swim, followed by a 24km run over 7 Munros, 11km kayak and 54km bike ride, I was told by countless people that it was impossible. I would never get it off the ground, and besides, the task was far too much for the average human being! I never listened to them, and 18 years later, thousands have taken part in the challenge, and it has raised over £9 million for amazing charities. Take this as proof that we have to have unstinting, unwavering faith that, come what may, our project will succeed. A crucial element of positiverosity is belief.

You cannot hope to achieve full positiverosity without also having the traits of trust, honesty, and commitment. I find that these are all very much interlinked, and essential to anything you do in life. Trust in yourself, but also in others. Remember 'Commitment means doing the thing you said you'd do, long after the mood you said it in has left you.' How many times have you been let down after someone committed to something? It happens all the time. Don't let yourself be the one who lets you down by wavering. Honesty is also paramount: the only power you truly have in this life is your word and how cheaply you use it. Think before you commit to something, say what you're going to do, and then do it. Before I commit to anything – especially medium to large events! – I think long and hard before I give my answer because when I say yes, I will have to carry that promise through. Your word is your bond.

High motivation and fitness are also key traits to positiverosity. You need the motivation to get through the highs and lows of any endeavour. While going through selection I would never have been able to endure the relentless poor weather and various injuries I sustained while holding down my full-time job and keeping in touch with my family, without an enormous capacity to remain positive and motivate myself. The thing you're doing has to be really worth it: you have to be on fire with it, it being the one passion in your world. It depends on your endeavour, of course, but for passing SAS selection, it's imperative that you have high levels of fitness. I group this in with motivation, because you are required to do a huge amount of training *on your own*, quite separately from the weekends away. If you don't put in the physical effort, you will not make the strict timings, or be able to carry the huge loads. Training takes discipline. Make sure you have enough time to prepare. Prevent injury by warming up and stretching to minimise the risk of pulling muscles or tendons. Make sure you are in the best possible shape before you even start: selection will take any minor injury or weakness and make it a hundred times worse.

I have failed SAS selection, and I have passed it. What I can honestly say made all the difference, are the traits above. When I first tried to pass, I had no idea of the notion of positiverosity, and in the end, I didn't have the mental strength and positive attitude I needed to complete the course. The second time, I was beginning to piece it together, and it changed the outcome. I hope that sharing it with you now will prevent you making the mistakes I did first time around, and give you all the tools you need to succeed at whatever endeavour is your personal passion.

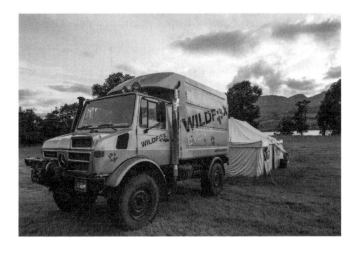

So, I had passed selection. I'd undertaken it willingly, knowing exactly what it entailed and I had prevailed. However, having succeeded in this challenge and joined the squadron I was now committed to 'continuation' with its many rigorous training weekends. Combining this with a day job and building up my own business (then called Events and Activies Ltd) meant that I was working absolutely flat out. Energy and commitment are funny things! If we diversify our energy too much by attempting too many projects, we dilute our power and are rarely successful at anything. I could see this in practice in the reserve regiment I joined. Generally, if you work for the civil service or government departments you are given generous paid leave. However, if you work for a small employer or were self-employed, then it becomes very hard to keep all the plates spinning at once. I believe that in life, we must focus on one main project, and put all our energy into that project if we are to be successful. I loved being part of the regiment but as the months went by I was becoming increasingly aware that my long term game plan was to develop my own events business, and I could not let go of this dream. I knew in my heart that that was where my true passion lay, and I had to practice positiverosity and commit to it full-time.

It all began with the Caledonian Challenge. As the business grew and grew, I set my sights further and further, but for now, this one event was all that mattered. Nothing like it existed in Scotland at the time, and it was very much a pioneering, high-risk adventure full of unknowns, experimentation, and (with a lot of luck) rewards. Remembering the MacLehose Trailwalker, I thought, if it worked in Hong Kong, why couldn't it work here? Yes, there were midges, and yes, the weather was often ghast-

ly, but we had 20 hours of daylight on the longest day in June, so midsummer was set as the date.
When I did the MacLehose Oxfam Hong Kong
Trailwater in 1995, I had no idea that two years later
I'd be embarking on a career in organising events
like it. I tried to remember how it had worked: the
route had spanned from one end of the New Territories to the other. The 4000 people taking part
walked 100k in 30 hours – in 1995 I had compet-
ed with four friends and completed the route in
under 24 hours so as to double the money I raised
for Oxfam. I remembered the army provided very
basic support – tea and coffee, but not much else.
Our own support team of friends had met us at the
various checkpoints, and this is what gave us the
boosts of morale we needed as we got even more
exhausted at every checkpoint we reached. It had
been a great insight into a new world of outdoor
challenge and adventure, totally invigorating, with
everyone in the highest of spirits, delighted to be
out of the big city and putting themselves through
the ultimate challenge of their lives. It was decided that the Caledonian Challenge would be based
on similar lines, and support Highland communities, so in effect, participants would be challenging
themselves in the stunning Highlands while giving
back to many worthy causes throughout Scotland,
and I worked with the Scottish Community Foundation to make this happen.

I was on a roller coaster, and I loved it. Everything had to be learned from scratch: though I had passed SAS selection, I had no degree in outdoor education or mountain leadership. What I needed to know, I taught myself. Besides, how complicated could it be? A great lesson in life is to keep things as simple as possible. I still had doubts, of course: Who would want to travel to Scotland from London? Who would be willing to walk so far, and for so long? Would anyone want to raise money for Scottish causes, if they weren't Scottish? Would people pay the £120 to register and raise the further £400 required for the charity? What would happen if the weather was foul and the midges ghastly? What if no-one signs up?? I call this the inner chattering. Positiverosity means getting a grip on this, and turning every negative into a positive. Remember that positive affirmation is a hundred times more powerful than negative affirmation. Go back to your early childhood and ponder for a moment on the principles on which you were brought up. I was lucky and had very positive parents. Even with a confident upbringing, the doubts and self-critical thoughts are still there. The key is how we overcome them, using the power of positive thinking to move forward and be successful at catching those negative internal chatterings and changing them.

The main thing, in the end, is to just start. Start small, perhaps, but just start. Remember the

Goethe principle, about 'all outside influences moving your way when there is belief and faith in your mission'. During the development of the Caledonian Challenge, I took matters into my own hands, and spent weeks and months visiting prospective teams in their offices to present the Challenge. I compiled a 45-minute presentation, with an 8-minute DVD, an event run-through and a few minutes on training and preparation. I had between 15 and 50 people in each presentation. This is how the business was built. Angus introduced me to a group of influential business leaders (the Caledonian Challenge Advisory Board) who in turn put me in contact with potential participants to present to – then the hard slog was down to me. To my knowledge, nobody else in the industry does this, spends the endless hours travelling and speaking in order to draw attention to their cause. It was positiverosity that gave me this determination, my one key advantage. At the end of it all, in my first year, over 500 people signed up for the 1999 Caledonian Challenge.

Twenty years on, not only has the Caledonian Challenge become a household name, it has pioneered this type of adventure challenge in the UK and raised over £14 million for communities throughout Scotland through the Scottish Community Foundation. Over 18,000 people have taken part in the gruelling non-stop 54-mile challenge

down the West Highland Way, from the foot of Ben Nevis to the banks of Loch Lomond. Just think for a moment of the overall impact of this event, the millions of hours of training undertaken by all those walkers, making new friends, bonding office teams, potentially saving lives as people improve their fitness levels. Then there is the impact on the lives of not only the participants, but those who've benefited from the funds raised. Then, there are the thousands of volunteers, families, friends, charity supporters and other personnel who've been involved. Then think about the massive logistical operation in setting it all up and looking after up to 1600 participants per year, one thousand support team members in 500 support vehicles, 200 marshals, and volunteers over a 24-hour period through the night. It all started with an idea, an idea full of belief, faith, confidence, can do, planning, determination, and positiverosity. Looking back, it seems like a massive risk. Fear and worry could have easily killed the idea off. That is why this book is so important because I have been there and experienced first hand what it takes to make it happen. Was it stressful? You bet. Were there moments of tumultuous despair, worry and drama? Absolutely. Where there moments when I wanted to jack it all in and take an easy low risk job option? No, because I had factored in all this worry and fear stuff as part of the deal. When things don't go well, people let you down, marquees get blown away in storms, generators fail, support teams have serious car accidents, the weather throws thunder and lightning at you – the list goes on and on – you deal with this in a calm and effective manner. You learn to keep calm and carry on. In life, we are continuously weighing up the risk/reward factor and increasingly we are becoming more risk-averse in all areas of life. Our society is rapidly turning into a nanny state. Humans are not being stretched as much as we should, and thus the grit and resilience are no longer there. Schools are taking lesser risks with outdoor pursuits. Education should be about gaining the confidence to be positive and having a go, striving and taking risks because the rewards are so much greater if we do. The Caledonian Challenge is an example of an idea turned into reality with a massive long term impact. From the Caledonian Challenge WildFox Events went on to develop a further 18 major events raising over £40 million for charities worldwide.

POINTS FOR REFLECTION

- A positive thought is 1000 times more powerful than a negative thought.

- Be selective when watching, reading or listening to news, 99% of which is negative and which will dramatically effect your positive mental attitude.

- Every situation can be turned into a positive.

- Always look for the good and positive in every person.

- Only mix with people who will support your plans and objectives and back you up in a positive manner.

- Keep away from all negative influences.

- Repeat positive affirmations of your goals, plans and projects twice daily.

- If you are positive you will attract good things and if you are negative you will attract bad outcomes.

- Always expect the best and that is what you will receive.

- Believe in your own powers to accomplish.

- Expel fear.

- Your mental concept is all that matters.

- Focus your desires into one great dominating desire.

- Leap and the net will appear.

- To keep the body in good health is a duty otherwise we will not be able to keep our mind strong and clear.

- Healthy body, healthy mind.

- I hear and I forget. I see and I remember. I do and I understand.

- Opportunity is missed by most people because it is dressed in overalls and looks like work.

- To allow yourself to be happy is the greatest wisdom there is.

- A kind word is better than the best gift

- The wise laugh often and much and find at least one reason to laugh each day even if it's not at themselves.

CHAPTER 6
PERSEVERANCE – THE ULTRA-TRAIL DU MONT BLANC

PERSEVERANCE: the endurance to see your goals through to the bitter end.

How should we deal with setbacks? What if some things don't go to plan? In this chapter I'll tell you how to keep going, even when the going gets tough. Perseverance means having courage and belief in yourself, even though the road may be long. When I completed the Ultra-Trail du Mont Blanc, it was sheer perseverance that got me to the end.

Closely related to the idea of passion, is that of perseverance. Once you have discovered your passion – what you would do if you were not paid, what burns in your heart and provides the energy to drive forward all your actions – you must combine it with a strong will to take control and be the master of your own destiny. In order to follow your true calling, it is necessary to override all obstacles. If you have passion without perseverance, you will never achieve what you set out to do, because your ideas will never get off the ground. If you have perseverance without passion and a true belief in your mission, you will struggle and fail in your endeavours.

Perseverance was a crucial element of my completing the Ultra-Trail du Mont Blanc in 2007. The Ultra-Trail du Mont Blanc, or UTMB, is an ultramarathon, taking place in the Alps and following the route of the Tour du Mont Blanc, starting and finishing at Chamonix. The route is the equivalent of completing four full 26.2-mile marathons and climbing Mount Everest at the same time, with a distance of 163 kilometres and 9000 metres of ascent. The overall cut off time in 2007 was 46 hours, with regular cut off points along the way, with only 29 refreshment and check-in stations. Competitors were not allowed to have supporters helping throughout, and had to make do with the provisions provided, which were adequate but consisted mainly of tea, coffee, noodle soup, cheese, salami, biscuits, chocolate and water. Some stops just had water, others just check-in monitors. We were also allowed to deposit two bags of extra kit at Courmayeur (77 kilometres along the route) and at Champex-Lac (122 kilometres along the route).

I had attempted the event in 2006, but had been unaware of the mid-course cut off times and infuriatingly had been withdrawn halfway through due to being late. I wasn't giving up on my aspiration to complete the course, and I vowed that 2007 would be the year I'd conquer it. 2007 was also a remarkably busy year for my company, with me spending most of my time coaxing people into signing up for one or more of our team charity events. I therefore felt it was appropriate for me to set my own personal challenge as an act of good faith, registering for the UTMB as the ultimate test. I was keen to practice what I preached at all those endless presentations up and down the country. Despite being so difficult, the event is also hugely popular, with all 2400 places being taken two days after registration opened in December 2006.

I must confess that my preparation was not what it should have been. Life was busy, the company was doing well, and my wife Jo and I had a young family with two daughters then aged 3 years and 15 months respectively. I had great difficulty fitting in a training regime appropriate for the immense challenge ahead. My training was sporadic and inconsistent and mostly consisted of combining training with taking our two new employees through our full portfolio of challenges, from the Rob Roy to Maggie's Bike and Hike. My longest training session consisted of taking a kayak one mile across Loch Tay, with my beloved black spaniel Mungo, and running/walking six Munros followed by running 15 miles home, all in 12 hours. To my dismay, I also learned during this time that the route had been extended that year, from 156 kilometres to 163, the organisers having been persuaded by the mayor of Saint-Gervais that the event should also take in the historic spa town. An area of preparation I did manage well was arriving in Chamonix, along with my wife, daughters and a brace of parents-in-law, four days before the start of the event, which allowed me to become acclimatised to the altitude. Three days before kick off, I went for a 12-mile run from Vallorcine, up to a height of 2400 metres, and strongly advise anyone thinking of participating in this event to travel out a few days beforehand to get used to the altitude and become familiar with the terrain.

Registration at the main sports complex in Chamonix was well organised and efficient. We were given a thorough kit check, competitor number, special microchip on a wrist band and an update on changes or problems with the route. I purchased two long graphite walking poles (not telescopic ones, as they tend to break easily) and a special endurance rucksack with side and belt pouches. This also contained a three-litre camel back reservoir with tube. We all had to carry two head torches and two sets of spare batteries, together with waterproofs, pantaloons (tight running Lycra trousers), thermals, a hat, a first aid kit, a whistle and emergency rations.

On August 28th, 2007, at 6pm, 2400 runners from all over the world congregated in Chamonix's central square, accompanied by rousing music and dramatic speeches. The weather was absolutely perfect, as the sun had dipped behind the spectacular mass of Mont Blanc and the awe-inspiring Glacier des Bossons and Taconnaz. The countdown took place – and we were off. It took me ten minutes to cross the starting line, as I was determined not to get caught up in the typical rush of adrenaline that occurs when you have thousands of cheering spectators to show off to. The atmosphere was electric, with all 2400 of us setting off on an incredible adventure, not knowing what was ahead of us. My determination to complete the course was stronger than ever, and I was itching to go.

The first 8 kilometres of the course, towards the ski resort of Les Houches, were flat, and provided the perfect gradual warm up before our first major hill – La Charme, at 1793m (we had been issued with map charts showing all the distances, names of villages, check points, cut off times, heights and altitudes of the course – a bit like those programmes on the running machines in your local gym, except this was a 46-hour programme, not a 30-minute one). We were already two hours into the event, and very few of us seemed to be talking. You could feel the concentration and determination in the air, and hear our heavy breathing and the tapping of hundreds of sticks on the paths as we ascended out of the first valley. By now it was dark, and hundreds of head torches sparkled and twisted up and over the La Charme ridge. Groups were standing to one side, changing into warmer clothing, teams adjusting their kit, putting on head torches and peeing into the bushes (I felt sorry for the female competitors – only 7% of the field – who usually had to disappear into the undergrowth for a pee). At 14km into the event, I remember looking back down towards Chamonix from La Charme and thinking that I still had 44 hours of non-stop running, walking, climbing and descending ahead of me. 'Stick to it, perseverance, pace yourself David.'

The mind is an extraordinary thing! It's so easy to catch the herd mentality, always trying to keep up with others, or feeling like you're dropping behind. The mind plays games, with its cautious, considerate side balanced by its brutal, no-nonsense, I-will-finish-come-what-may side. There is also the chattering side of the mind and its continuous questioning. Am I drinking enough? Is that a blister starting? How are the others getting on? Am I warm enough? Then, it'll go off on a tangent and start thinking of something far away, family, work, events. Being aware of my lack of training also preyed on my thoughts, making me worry about how my heart would be coping 30 hours into the event, after the fourth massive summit. All that got me through it was constantly reminding myself that 50% of the field would not make it to the finish line, and that it was all about energy conservation, mental control, a positive attitude, and an awareness of one's energy levels at all times.

At 20 kilometres we hit our second food and refreshment stop at Saint-Gervais-les-Bains, a 1000m descent from La Charme. It was nice to reacquaint oneself with civilisation, and get some encouragement from the hundreds of locals, supporters and staff lining the streets. It was so easy, once again, to get caught up in the exhilarating atmosphere and temporary lift of spirits, forgetting the grind along the route towards the next objective. The chattering mind takes over again: you imagine yourself stumbling over the finish line in Chamonix. Who will be there? My family? – No, you must focus on the next step, and then the next, and then the one after that. Any journey starts with the first step and then you break it down into lots more digestible chunks, otherwise the whole picture becomes too overwhelming. The one distraction I permitted myself was exchanging encouraging remarks with my fellow competitors – well done, bravo, *bonne chance*, good luck! It was difficult to hold a conversation, though, as we were all so focused, and my French is not brilliant.

At 10 hours on the track, and 49km in, Les Chapieux was a most welcome stop. It was still dark, and I was looking forward to some hot food. Noodle soup, bread, cheese, salami and four cups of coke did the trick, and I was up and off again after a 10-minute break. I was already wary of the cut off times, determined not to repeat my mistake of 2006, and although I was two hours ahead I knew I should keep going, fully aware that the cut offs would decrease further on, while I would become more exhausted and slow. A 1000m climb took me over the Col de la Seigne at 59k and into Italy. The sun was rising, and the views north into the Glacier de la Lee Blanche, and back west towards Les Chapieux were quite spectacular. Although I knew I still had a long way to go, it was difficult to not become immersed in the beauty of the pristine nature around me, and the euphoria of the moment.

I arrived at Elisabetta check point feeling great and still with two hours in the cut off bank – quite an achievement, considering this is where I was withdrawn the previous year. I had been on the hoof for 14 hours and covered 63km, with just another 500m ascent before the enormous descent of 1245m into Courmayeur. The descent was agony, as my right knee cap had slipped, but I found running downhill backwards made the experience less painful, although probably also less elegant. With the sun rising again, the heat was becoming intense, with zero wind as I trotted down into the sports centre at 11.38am. I have to admit, at 18 hours down, with 28 still to go and 93km to cover, the task was beginning to seem impossible. I felt totally exhausted, dehydrated, hungry and in need of a leg massage. The organisation at this checkpoint in Italy was pretty chaotic. We had to queue for 30 minutes to pick up our spare kit, the signage was non-existent and none of the marshals seemed to know where anything was. After more noodle soup, a bowl of pasta, a change of socks and T-shirt and a frustrating 20-minute wait for a pathetic tickle of a leg rub, I was out of the nightmare centre and back on my way. I'd hoped to catch 30 minutes of kip to combat my exhaustion, but alas, this luxury had been taken up with queueing.

Without sleep, climbing the 800m from Courmayeur to Rifugio Bertone in the searing mad-dogs-and-Englishmen heat was undoubtably the low point of the challenge. I passed at least 30 competitors heading back down the hill to Courmayeur, the heat having been too much. Watching their leisurely descent, I was so tempted to join them, but still more determined to keep going. We are continually battling with the inner voice of doubt, fear, and worry. We must learn to overrule these emotions with utter conviction and replace them continuously with Positiverosity.

It was there that the importance of perseverance became apparent to me, as well as the connection with perseverance and what I have come to think of as a 'why am I doing this?' factor. A week before flying to France to start the challenge, I realised I needed a better reason for doing this mad event than my personal desire to beat my achievement the year before, something to spur me in the darkest moments of my journey. I knew my body was capable of the challenge, having been through harder ordeals in the past, including SAS selection, but I also knew that my training had been gravely insufficient. So, I asked my brother-in-law Peregrine to nominate three charities that would benefit from my efforts. Peregrine had been diagnosed with cancer and had gone through a traumatic period of chemotherapy, so I was adamant to not let him, or the charities, down. I was right – in the end, this became my reason for sticking with it, and my defence against the sway of the mind. Every time its negative sides intervened, I was able to think of Peregrine and the charities to override the urge to give up, and kept moving forward.

Reaching Rifugio Bertone at 81km was a huge relief, and I couldn't resist finding some shel-

ter from the midday sun and resting for a while. The twenty minutes spent at Bertone, resting my aching limbs in the shade, provided a remarkable respite, and I was soon up and on my way with renewed vigour. It came at a price, however: aware of time running out, I ran on any flat or downhill terrain and walked swiftly when ascending. I checked into Rifugio Bonatti at 90km, and raced on the Arnuya at 93km, making the cut off by just 17 minutes. I had lost valuable time at Courmayeur and Bertone, and had nothing left in the reserve time bank. It was essential to check out before the final countdown, and those that remained at the checkpoint were asked to withdraw. Grabbing the usual slices of cheese, salami, biscuits and downing a further five cups of coke, I grabbed my sack and sticks, and just made it out before the checkpoint closed. I now faced one of the course's toughest climbs up to Grand Col Ferret, 2490m above sea level, and an 800m climb from Arnuya.

Two competitors en route to the summit of Grand Col Ferret on the Swiss border were airlifted off, and I never found out what happened to them. By now it was getting dark again, and we were beginning our second night in the mountains. 'Could I hitch a ride on that helicopter? Should I collapse and wait to be picked up?' 'No, be positive, keep going.' In some ways, I felt hopeless, as I knew I was at the back of the field, but I also had hope and was determined to continue. At time of adversity and despair we need a powerful force of inner conviction and perseverance to spur us on and drown out those negative demons. Surmounting the Col Ferret at 98km in, I had no time to stop – it was a race against time, and I had to just keep focusing on the next stage, and then the next. Luckily, this part of the course was a dream descent for 20km, before another major ascent up to Champex and Mount Bovine. Chamonix was a blur, and I had almost persuaded myself that Champex, at 122km, would be my limit. I felt positive about the conditions, as I preferred the nighttime stints, with the temperature cooler and more like Scotland's, and I love running downhill, so was able to make up time. The terrain, however, was slippery, and on one occasion I completely disappeared down a slope off the track and ended up in a thick thorn bush. The head torch I had was not brilliant at picking out all the bumps in the track, and this, combined with the severe fatigue and sleep deprivation I was experiencing, made it easy to fall prey to minor falls.

The moon, though, was shining, and for the first time I joined up with another runner, a Frenchman, and we chatted about a variety of subjects. This was great, as it distracted me from the monotony and fatigue of my long journey. It wasn't long, however, before we parted ways and I was back on my own to deal with my mental battles about reaching the next phase. 115km down, and I had overtaken over twenty runners on the descent. I was feeling OK, no blisters, still drinking Lucozade from my reservoir and eating little and often. Little and often is the key for endurance events: I had Honey Stinger gels, energy bars, oranges, apples, peanuts, chocolate, crisps, and water. Pounding through the woods, I came across a group standing over a collapsed runner. He refused to move and was just incapable of standing up. The medics had been called. A classic example of energy burnout. I was leading by example, and the mantras I set out in my presentations were flooding my mind. I was living through it firsthand. Never ask people to do something that you are not prepared to do yourself: the first basic rule of leadership.

The next two hours were vital to my completing the event. The negative thoughts were gradually overpowering the positive, 'will do', side of the mind. I met a German runner who had been in the event the previous year. He convinced me that we had run out of time and that there was no way we were going to reach Champex before the 3.30pm cut off. I was secretly relieved, and had mentally given up on continuing beyond that point. We walked together for a while, before I realised I had to shake him off. I had to jettison this chap's negative influence, and move ahead at a quicker pace. Do not be influenced by outside negative forces – say

'Is that so?', move on quickly and eradicate all negativity. I was checking my watch eagerly every five minutes during the exhausting ascent to Champex.

By now it had been 33 hours on the hoof, and I was desperate for some rest. Through the woods I began to hallucinate: 'Was that a giraffe?' 'No, it's a tree.' My mind began to ramble on, 'Keep going, keep moving, catch that person in front, overtake him, OK next person, run, hurry, focus!' I was really struggling, and had made up my mind to finish at Champex, when a fellow runner from Scotland called Jim Drummond (15 times a veteran of Scotland's toughest event, the 97-mile West Highland Way Race) overtook me with encouraging words. 'We can still make the cut off, but we have to start running!' When you find a positive force or influ-

ence, latch onto it and it will inspire renewed vigour and spirit. We started chatting as we climbed the steep hill, and it emerged that we had many mutual acquaintances back home. It was at that moment that the belief that I could finish the entire course was planted in my mind. Jim and I motivated and encouraged each other in our darkest moments, and it was remarkable how the conversation was able to take the pain and suffering out of the equation. We made the cut off by 14 minutes. Without time to change into any fresh kit (Champex being the second kit change area), it was a question of grabbing handfuls of food, filling our reservoirs and moving out of the checkpoint literally as the countdown had started.

I was now completely committed to finishing, and suddenly the dream of running through Chamonix across that finish line was becoming a reality. Positive affirmations began to flood my mind – 'I can do this,' 'I can raise more money for the charities,' 'I will not let Peregrine down!' It is extraordinary how the mind and morale shifts so radically from negative to positive in the presence of a friend who can motivate you to press on in moments of doubt and helplessness.

'Got to have a power nap!' shouted Jim as we started the arduous ascent of yet another mountain at 131km. Great idea! We stretched out in the grass at the side of the track and set an alarm for five minutes. What a difference those five minutes made! What a wonderful sensation to give those aching limbs and feet a rest. This new mountain, Bovine, was less a path than a rock climb, and Jim and I stumbled, slipped, swore, fumbled and tripped our way up 500m to the top. In my desperation I felt like Gollum frantically searching for 'my precious' Ring.

It was 7am as we approached the summit of Bovine and the sun was just rising. Thirty-seven hours, with still eight plus to go, and we now had to race down the hill to Trient to make the cut off for 8.30am. From the summit, we saw the village and relaxed our pace. We'd be in Trient with 15 minutes to spare. But, to our horror, we arrived at the village and were informed that the checkpoint was a further 3km down the valley. We shifted into semi-sprint mode – with not a moment to lose. We could see the checkpoint, but the track kept zigzagging away from it and the seconds were ticking by.

We made the checkpoint with less than five minutes to spare, grabbed food and water, and quickly checked out. We were now heading up the last major mountain (700m) to Catogne, back on the French border, and the 142km mark. The sun was beating down on us again, with no wind, and the track just kept winding up and up, into the clouds. Jim was slowing, and I kept ahead of him, always within sight to spur him on. He had helped me, and I was going to support him too, all the way to the finish. Along and over the top of Catogne we went, followed by the massive 740m descent into Vallorcine. Once again, the pressure was on. We had no time to rest, and as soon as the track flattened and dipped into France we took off, amid spectacular views north towards Lac d'Emosson and over to Mount Oreb (2645m above sea level). The adrenaline had now taken over: the thought of missing the next cut off in Vallorcine overrode the pain of all those miles.

After Argentière, the track seemed to go on forever, undulating up and down, another hill, another village, more woods, remote tracks, long fields. So close now, we were concerned about

missing the 46-hour cut off, the final hurdle, and used our last reserves of strength and willpower to quicken our pace. Finally, we were heading into the outskirts of Chamonix, round the parks, into the town centre, through the cheering crowds – and over the finish line! Jim and I had made it, crossing it together in the nick of time.

It was an extraordinary feeling. Not emotional, just an overwhelming sense of relief to have finished the course. We crossed the finish line in 45 hours, 5 minutes and 58 seconds. I came in 1393rd place. Just 1455 people completed the course that year, from the 2400 that started. The best part was seeing my family at the end – knowing that they would be at the finish line was what had inspired me to get there.

I know that retrospect is rose-tinted but looking back, I thoroughly enjoyed the experience, and raised over £8000 for some fantastic charities. I had achieved my goal, which was simply to complete the course. That said, I could hardly walk after the finish, my knees seized up, and I (surprisingly!) had a thoroughly restless night's sleep afterwards.

Even more valuable than my memories of the experience itself were the lessons it taught me about the nature and importance of perseverance. Endurance is much more a mental battle than a physical one. You truly are capable of anything you set your mind to – commitment, determination, and refusal to succumb to the negative part of your brain is what will make your dreams achievable. It's important not to get too excited when things go well, and not to get too down when they do not go well. Life consists of continuous ups and downs, the yin and yang of success and disappointment, love and hate, acceptance and rejection, well-being and depression, wealth and poverty. It is how we deal with these emotions that is so crucial. Remember, we are in life for the long term, we need solid foundations and emotional tools. Remember that habits are one of the most difficult things to change and it takes determination, resolve, belief and persistence to achieve the changes we desire. Whatever your challenge, make sure you have good reasons for completing it. Take away the get-out clauses and excuses, be determined to achieve your goals, and rely on a friend. Raise money for charity, or give yourself a mission. You need to know why you are doing this. You need to know who you are doing this for. The answer to the question 'is this really important to me?' needs to be YES. Without this passion, from which you can draw endless mental toughness, you will not persevere and you will not succeed.

POINTS FOR REFLECTION

- Commitment is doing the thing you said you would do long after the mood you said it in has left you.

- Make sure you know what you want before you commit.

- Take commitment seriously and only commit if you have the 100% will to see it through.

- Most people say one thing and do the opposite thus selling out on their only power. The only power you have is your word, so honour it.

- Start committing to the little things in life in preparation for the bigger things in life.

- Much rain wears the marble.

- Be consistent and persevere – never give up.

- Create fitness and mental tests – programmes to test your perseverance.

- Sign up for a marathon, join a chess club, find a way to test your mind.

- Radiate courage, health, strength, harmony and love.

- All power is absolutely under our own control.

- No totally honest person can say that they were always happy, life is made up of happy and sad moments. One cannot exist without the other just as there cannot be light without dark.

- Silent thought is after all the mightiest agent in human affairs.

- Don't ask what the world needs, ask what makes you come alive and go and do it, because what the world needs is people who have come alive.

CHAPTER 7
PASSION –
HOW TO FIND YOURS AND CREATE THE MOMENTUM YOU NEED TO ACHIEVE YOUR DREAMS

PASSION: A long-lasting, burning desire.
To be on fire with your vocation.

Finally, we come to passion, perhaps the most important tool of them all. It all starts here. In this chapter, I'm going to tell you how to find your passion, how to keep it alight, and how to channel it into results.

Can you remember a time in your life when you've been truly on fire with a passion, a red hot energy that propelled you to action? I hope you have. To live without passion is to never achieve your full potential. However, if you have had that passion, have you let it wane? If you don't take care to fan the flames of your desire, it will sputter and die. Our minds are like changing chameleons. How do we stop ourselves from getting distracted, from moving on to the next thing? Life is big, complicated, and messy. Sometimes you may feel as if it is doing everything in its power to drive you off course. To plan for the long term, we must be obsessed, consumed, and absolutely passionate about our goal, or the dream, well, it just won't last.

By now you've read about how I completed SAS selection which gave me the resolve, perseverance and self-belief to build the Caledonian Challenge into a fundraising force for good. All great endeavours start with an idea and WildFox began on a crazy mountain-climbing adventure with my friend Angus MacDonald. This lit the fire of passion within me and I've managed to sustain that passion for over twenty years. I built up my business and created spectacular, challenging events throughout the UK and Europe in support of many wonderful local, national and international charities. Some of these events have become household names – the ripples have spread around the globe and I'll wager that you'll either know someone who's taken part in one of them, or who has benefitted from one of the charities supported. Since I set out to build that first mass participation Caledonian Challenge I have created more than eighteen major events over twenty years, which have raised over £40 million for charity. I could never have foreseen the remarkable journey my life would take me on before I discovered my passion, but I could also never have achieved such extraordinary things without it. Passion is pure energy, motivation and inspiration.

Once it has you in its clutches, it has the power to change everything.

The principles in this book have been the principles I have used every day to make WildFox a success. I judge my own success by the impact I have on the world – this has been my passion all along and this is my reward. Yes, there have been ups and downs, but at the end of the day the principles remain the same. The words of advice I seek to share through these principles are for you to consider in the light of your own chosen passion. Follow your own road map, be determined, and you will be successful. Success is not easy – if it was, think how many people would be out achieving their dreams right now! There will be disappointments, upsets, and setbacks. Success is about how you handle these roadblocks when they arise. Remember what Isaac Newton said when he discovered gravity: 'What goes up, must come down.' The course of life may ebb and flow like a tide, the wheel of fortune may turn, and yin and yang become unbalanced. Failure is part of the rich tapestry of life; embrace failure as part of your individual journey to success. If you have not failed at anything, you surely have not even tried anything! Learn to recognise your failures, learn from them, fail, move on, and fail better next time. There have been plenty of failures and disappointments in my journey, and I am not ashamed of them. They each taught me a lesson, which I am sharing with you in this book. My purpose with this book is to inspire you to make the changes necessary so that you can go forward and make the best of your life. My desire is to bring out your passions and ignite something within you to take you in a new direction of positivity and inspiration.

How do we attract this passion, this so-called burning desire? How do we know if we are actually doing the right thing? How do we test our passion credentials? How do we get inspired? What is true inspiration? These are very tricky questions. We all have different desires and passions, depending on our age and experiences. Finding your passion is also about timing. If Angus MacDonald had not offered me the opportunity to go out with him that day, I would be doing something completely different with my life! Yes, I may have found passion in another field – but I may not have! At the time, I was 34 years old, without a passion. All I had wanted at the time was to move back to Scotland from London, and had been offered a job as a marketing manager for a small communications company. I sometimes imagine how my life might have turned out – I would have been happy at Kindrochit, yes, and happy enough in my job. Happy *enough* is not what I think we each deserve to find in life. To my mind, a life well-lived is one of more intensity, more excitement, more risk and nerve, in which one dares oneself to put it all out there and do the thing that sets the heart on fire.

So why is it that so few people are truly passionate about what they do during their lives? For me, it connects with the idea of a purpose. Whenever I feel down and inclined to give up I've had my experiences to reflect on, combined with an awareness of the deep humanitarian injustices I see in the world. Exposing oneself and engaging in such injustice is always enough to inspire a passion for change and doing good. Every time I visit a charity project overseas or in the UK my passion is reignited and reaffirmed. It is an opportunity to renew my resolve to continue doing what I'm doing. I only have to look back at pictures of the schools in Malawi with 'supported by the Artemis Great Kindrochit Quadrathlon' written with pride on the walls and think of all those children spanning the world eating and learning at school because of one madcap day in the Scottish Highlands to know that all the effort has been worth it a thousand fold.

So, how can we create this passion? Young people nowadays are setting out into a very competitive, aggressive, un-gentlemanly, ruthless society. Perhaps I wouldn't blame them for choosing the safe option over their true passion. So what can we instil in their thought processes about passion? What can we impart? How can we motivate, inspire and ignite the thought processes that become part of our way of being, so that the important princi-ples of life and ethics are instilled within us?

One way is to strive continually to reach the higher plane of creativity. We need to build up a bank of affirmations that we can tap into, a bank of things, experiences, moments of enlightenment, moments of love and generosity, and glimmers of inspiration. We need to capture these moments in our consciousness and treasure what triggers them. It might take time to dissolve what I call the stink-ing thinking – the negativity. It comes down to continuous, repetitive, positive affirmations, and letting them lift you onto a more productive and more creative train of thought.

My positive affirmations are triggered by:
Being in my secret garden of peace
Walking in the hills with my dogs and family
Listening to inspiring music
Running in the hills
Driving through beautiful scenery
Kayaking along the banks of Loch Tay
Exploring the Himalayas

What are your triggers? Stop right here and write them down.

How do we find our passion? You may already be well along the road with your passion, or you may be young, lacking in experience and seeking direction. If so, I cannot tell you what your passion is. That is something each of us must seek within ourselves. A good place to start is to ask yourself what it is you enjoy doing most. Do you like baking and meeting new people? Open a bakery! Enjoy making art and seeing the world? Become a photojournalist! For me, the things I enjoy most are being outdoors, inspiring people to get outside, and trying to make the world a better place for others. These three touchstones are the foundations of WildFox Events. If you can't think of something you really enjoy doing, I would advise you to try as many vocations and things as possible. When we are young, and at school, we really have no clue what we want to do, yet we are set various subjects depending on what our parents have suggested or what we *think* we might want to do – but how do we know we might like something until we have tried it for ourselves? I believe so many people go through life in the wrong vocation, because they start out on a course and are either too afraid to change, or are simply unable to, due to family ties, commitments, or a myriad of other reasons. I ask you this – what is better, staying safe in something that may make you content, or taking a risk to chase your true heart's desire? We only have one life! Don't waste it – we must be passionate about what we do, even if it takes years to find our passion!

I have begun to spend time at schools in China, speaking about the WildFox philosophy, and on a recent visit, a student asked me what they should do if they didn't enjoy their subjects. My answer? 'Change them, and follow your passion every time!' To all young people, I say try as many things as possible, take a year out, travel the world, work in different places, learn new languages, meet different people, experience other cultures, try new kinds of food, explore, have adventures, climb mountains, work in bars, go on treks, work with charities and experience life to the full! After all, once you get a full-time job, secure a mortgage and become laden down with life's other entrapments and entanglements, you are stuck, and that youthful, inquisitive, adventurous, creative self is stifled and the urge to explore gradually becomes extinguished. Take a year out after school, and even another one after university. This will give you time to really test your passions, so that you can experience more and have a better chance of following a more fulfilling course later in life. Be open to opportunities! We all feel scared sometimes, but don't be afraid to try something different. Above all, don't blinker yourself. Focus is great, but not when it stops you from seeing the great opportunities that could be right there in front of you.

But, once we have found our passion, how do we keep it burning within us? How can we stay positive, keep the doubts from creeping in, stay motivated and keep the passion fresh in our hearts? A big part of sustaining passion is in finding equilibrium. Think about the yin and yang of life, the light and dark, balanced in harmony. When I think of balance, I think of the changing water level of Loch Tay with the turning seasons, the high water and the low, and the equilibrium in between. Does this not resemble life in general? For us, balance can be about not getting too overexcited, or too stressed. Chaos is unsustainable – to persist, and succeed, passion must be channelled into balance, like a long-term love affair that will get you through thick and thin. I always wondered, why do so many people fall for drugs and alcohol? And then I realised: because they are unhappy. They are not satisfied with their lot, they hate their job, the place where they live, their life! Drugs and alcohol provide that escape from a reality that is dulled by a lack of passion. Young people are especially vulnerable. They look for direction and reassurance through companionship but to achieve self belief and confidence they should avoid the company of those who numb their faculties and reduce their drive through drug use or excessive alcohol.

Don't get too excited when things go well, and don't get too down when they do not. Life consists of continuous ups and downs, but it is how we deal with these fluctuations that is crucial. Remember, we are in life for the long haul, and life is exciting and complicated. We need solid foundations and emotional tools to handle it. I wouldn't have succeeded in setting up WildFox Events without my SAS selection and the skills, self-belief, positive mindset and mental strength it gave me. Habits are one of the most difficult things to change, and it takes determination, resolve, belief, persistence and autosuggestion to achieve the changes we desire.

Another way to sustain your passion is to use what I call the future time zone. When going through particularly challenging circumstances, put your mind into a future mode and switch off. For example, when I was enduring selection with the SAS, there came a time when my body was aching for relief, respite, escape, rest and comfort. I knew that I was being tested to my absolute limit. I was cold, hungry, exhausted and hopeless, near to giving up. Instead of giving up, I switched my mind into a different zone and time frame, using my imagination to visualise myself in a more relaxing environment. I imagined myself on my boat with my beautiful black spaniel Mungo, soaring over the waters of Loch Tay on a sunny day, with not a cloud in the sky nor my mind. I tried to inhabit once again the feeling of total peace, love and tranquillity I felt in that moment. In doing this, I took myself away from the pain and stress of my current situation in the middle of a peat bog in the Brecon Beacons, and into a different thought process and zone. When you can't see a way out, hit the refresh button in your mind. So often we become stressed out and tangled up in our thinking. Think of a situation in which you were perfectly happy, and use it to ground yourself through the more difficult times.

When you are young, anything is possible. Passion means getting out there, seizing the adventure, exploring, risking it all, and living freely. Consider the simple enthusiasm of dogs. When life gets complicated, and I feel adrift from my passions, I take a long walk watching my springer spaniels covering the ground, always optimistic that they will find something new to explore. Their shorter lives condense our own experiences, and by sharing our time with them, we see a distillation of what is important in life. The older dog stays by my side, stepping aside to let the young whipper snapper do all the darting around, inspecting every tree. What amazing energy the younger dog has – the old boy was the same in his youth. My point, I suppose, is that this is the cycle of life, and pursuing and achieving your goals takes extraordinary energy and effort. You only live once, so don't let your energetic time pass without doing something you believe in.

Do we become wiser with age and should we expect youth to listen to experience, or must each generation find out for themselves? Can others learn from our advice and mistakes? If my twelve-year-old says she wants to climb Everest, swim the Channel or be the first girl in the SAS should we encourage this vibrant enthusiasm or do we temper it, knowing as we do with age the dangers that such endeavours entail? At what point does this light of adventure, risk and challenge get stamped out of us? And does it really matter? Maybe I'm not physically capable of some of the feats I did in my youth anymore, and that does sadden me. However, another part of my passion has always been to encourage the desire for adventure in others, and that part of me continues to flourish. Passion may change as we grow older, start families and find new direction and priorities but that doesn't necessarily mean you will lose touch with your original goals. Every new person who signs up to a WildFox event gives me the same thrill of excitement as when I participate in a challenge myself. My passion for WildFox burns as brightly as it did on that day with Angus striking out across the hills to conquer 32 Munros in four days.

At the end of the day, my one true desire is to leave a legacy that will inspire and motivate future generations to pick up the mantle and continue to strive for the good of humanity. I try to live by the wise words of Prentice Mulford: 'The aspiration, the earnest prayer or demand to be better, to have more power, to become more refined, will bring more and more of the finer elements and forces; that is spirit to you. But the motive must be the natural heart-felt zealous wish to impart what you receive to others.' Maybe I can't measure the overall impact WildFox Events has had on the world, whether that's through the money we've raised, or lives prolonged by increased exercise, but that's not the point. The overall objective is to make a positive impact on as many souls as possible, whether or not we know them. Just to know that the effort we are putting in will have an effect at the other end of the country, or even the other side of the planet, is humbling enough!

Many would argue that humanitarian causes are helped enough. Our government pays vast sums to help with various global crises through the Department for International Development – shouldn't that be sufficient? Why should we do more? To that I say, just look around you. It's clearly not enough. Day after day we witness humanitarian disaster after disaster, with millions of people suffering unspeakable deprivations, war, starvation, drought and disease. It is impossible for us to ignore it. This is why visiting the charities that WildFox Events supports is so important to me – it keeps the fire of my passion burning, each time renewing my determination to do everything in my power to help. After all, where we are born in this world is a lottery! Had we been born in a different part of the world or in a different time we would be in the same position!

The Syrian crisis has sucked in enormous resources from all major NGOs, but this means many other parts of the world have been neglected. Through our Artemis Great Kindrochit Quadrathlon event we have raised over £9 million in support of Mercy Corps, who are currently the biggest NGO operating in Syria, ahead of the United Nations. I believe that true understanding and compassion can only be stirred when one has visited these situations first-hand. I visited Malawi to get a sense of the circumstances there, and to see how the money raised from my events was making a tangible difference, and the experience was humbling, awe-inspiring, and instilled in me the drive to keep going with the events.

The first charity we went to visit was Mary's Meals, who were running a feeding programme in schools in Malawi. The Quadrathlon is responsible for feeding up to 10,000 children a year. Did you know it costs just £13.90 to feed a child for an entire year at school? Awesome! I was fortunate enough to visit six schools and meet the Mary's Meals volunteers, teachers and children. The deprivation they were living with made me think of my own comfortable life with my family back home, and it really hit home to me how desperate the situation is for so many families, who literally spend their entire day scraping together enough for one meal. One really begins to understand the importance of something as simple as a cup of nutritious porridge (like the 'magic porridge pot' of the children's story!), which helps both with keeping the children healthy and encourages them to attend school. This is the aim of Mary's Meals, to help children to receive an education and become more likely to get out of the cycle of poverty, and support their family better in the long term.

In the short term, though, Mary's Meals also works to deliver back packs to all schools where they provide meals. Each pack contains all the basic requirements a family might need, including a toothbrush, toothpaste, a towel, pens and paper, toys, flip flops, hairbrushes and other items – items which we wouldn't even think of in the western world – all packed with love and care by thousands of children who've had a better chance in life. Many of the schools we visited in Malawi lacked basic facilities like clean water, desks, classrooms and toilets, and this was evident by the childrens' reactions on receiving their back packs. It was remarkable! The screams of delight and joy were like it was a thousand Christmases all at once. It was incredibly moving to see how excited the children were about such simple items, especially compared to how my own children might have reacted. They shared their items, swapped them, played with them, and were so happy and animated that the headteacher had to let them go home! I will never forget the smiles on their faces.

The Martin Currie Rob Roy Challenge – another of our events – has also supported Malawi through Water Aid and I was able to visit them in Malawi and learn about how they work to provide much-needed sanitation and water projects all over the country. We witnessed a new well being opened in a village where the community had been walking miles to find water. Again, their joy and elation at having easily accessible clean water – something we take for granted every day – was humbling to witness.

On the third day, I visited Habitat for Humanity, also supported through the Rob Roy Challenge, which helps communities work together to build houses for struggling families. Then, on day four, we visited Sight Savers International, where they were working at a hospital to provide cataract operations. Imagine being able to restore someone's eyesight for as little as £16 per eye! Amazing, and incredibly inspiring, especially when I discovered that my great-grandfather, Arthur Sinclair, pioneered the cataract operation from his practice in Edinburgh. Arthur, the son of a minister on the banks of Loch Tay developed a way of restoring sight to the blind. It's kind of Biblical, and living as

I do on Loch Tay reminds me that everything in life is connected.

The time I spent in Malawi was an incredible experience, and when I got home I realised the visits had turned on a switch of inspiration. I couldn't forget what I had seen there, and there is so much more that we could do to help if we spent less time engrossed in our own lives and realised how easy it is to make a difference, and how many lives can be changed for the better by the smallest things. I greatly admire Magnus Macfarlane Barrow, who founded Mary's Meals over fourteen years ago. The charity now feeds 1.3 million children every day at a place of learning in over 15 countries. 93p from every pound donated goes to the feeding programme, and just 7p on admin and governance! How inspiring is that? Hundreds and thousands of local mums, aunties and grannies volunteer their time to prepare the food, which keeps the cost down. They have a vested interested in ensuring their children get a nutritious meal at school every day, so it really is such a simple concept, but it works so well, and is delivered with such love, care, compassion and passion.

There are still 54 million children out there not getting their meal at school, so we have a long way to go. Yet we have to start somewhere! Think of the little girl who threw one star fish back into the sea. 'What's the point?' said her father. 'What difference will it make?' 'It made a difference to that one!' the girl replied.

It is easy to become numb to the endless crises that happen all over the world. When we hear of another disaster, another war, another famine on the news, we switch off and get on with our lives, believing that our government will deal with the issues. However, at the end of the day, the government has fallen far short of the mark, and as individuals we must take responsibility, and do what we can to tackle poverty worldwide. We must take individual collective responsibility for our world.

This is what fuels the fire of my passion, but all I am able to offer is the story of my experiences and where they have led me. We are all different, and whatever we end up doing, there is no right or wrong way to live a life. At the end of the day, the vital question, the one that could change your life, turns out to be pretty straightforward: Are you passionate about what you're doing? If yes, great! If not, *change*. We are only on this planet for a short time, so make the most of it!

POINTS FOR REFLECTION

- Live in the now. Happiness is a now experience.

- Be passionate about everything you do.
  How do we turn our passion into a reality?

- Try out lots of things until you find your passion.

- Love mixed with passion is the most invincible combination known to mankind.

- What can we do that will cultivate a long-lasting burning passion?

- To have a passion you must develop a burning desire otherwise it will not last.

- Cultivate a white hot burning desire and be on fire with what ever you decide to do.

- Think intensively of the project/challenge in mind.

- Passion test: If you are passionate you would do what you do even if you weren't paid for it.

- Happiness is found in 'doing' not only in 'possessing'.

- I can be what I will to be.

- It is not will but desire that rules the world.

- Nothing great has ever been achieved without enthusiasm.

- Never has the world needed so much passion, love and understanding.

- Concentrate and become absorbed.

- A loving heart is the truest wisdom.

- Cultivate your imagination, desire, emotions and intuitional faculties, concentrate on the objective of your passion which you can then impress upon your subconscious mind.

CHAPTER 8
PUTTING THESE PRINCIPLES INTO PRACTICE, DON'T DREAM IT DO IT.

ADVENTURE: An unusual, exciting and daring experience.

I was in London en route to a meeting, when I received a call from Adam, who I had not seen for years. 'Fancy a crack at re-enacting *the Cockleshell Heroes* down the Gironde next August?' And where exactly might the Gironde be? I enquired. Within five minutes I had committed. Once I commit to something, there is no get-out clause.

I had committed to a re-enactment of one of the most audacious and daring British raids of World War II, a raid that was incredibly important for Allied morale when the Germans were at the height of their might in Europe in 1942. The original mission, codenamed 'Operation Frankton', was a daring plan to attack German cargo ships moored in the Port of Bordeaux, a main docking area for vessels supporting the German war effort. The team numbered 13 men in 6 canoes (codenamed 'cockles') and was concocted by Major Herbert 'Blondie' Hasler, who personally led the mission – a real hero. The plan was for the specially selected commandos to be taken to the Gironde estuary in Aquitaine, France, by submarine. In the pitch dark of a December night, they were to paddle 60 miles (97km) up the Gironde estuary to the port city of Bordeaux, somehow avoiding the 32 *Kriegsmarine* ships which patrolled the area, where they would fix limpet mines to docked German ships, and then escape southwards on foot to Spain. Of the thirteen, one team's canoe was damaged at the point of launching from the submarine, six were caught by the Germans and executed, and two men died of hypothermia, their canoe sinking in the cruel cross winds and fierce tides. Two – Hasler and his teammate – survived.

You may well have seen the famous 1955 film *The Cockleshell Heroes*, well, I had, and it seemed jolly exciting to re-enact it, as well as personally meaningful to me. Two of the men I most greatly admire are my grandfathers, both war veterans. I've already talked about Billy Fox-Pitt who I knew well, but my mother's father David Scrymgeour Wedderburn, who died so young at Anzio, is only known to me through my Granny Pat's stories. She died aged 102, and her memories went with her of a lost generation of young men full of their own dreams and schemes. We have some wonderful recordings of him playing the piano which I treasure. He was a very funny and talented impersonator and by all accounts a charming man. How I would like to have met him. I think the suffering experienced by that generation is something we need to value more highly today. Quiet resolve, 'Blitz Spirit' and 'the Spirit of Dunkirk', ordinary people displaying immense bravery in the face of tyranny are distinctly underrated values in a very immodest modern society! It seems to me that we've forgotten the sacrifices they made for us, which we should respect by trying to keep up the best of their old-fashioned values. To me, my grandfathers were true gentlemen. Not the kind who just hold doors open, drink whisky and keep a 'stiff upper lip'. Truly gentlemanly behaviour means standing up for those who are weak, and stoicism throughout difficulty. Recreating the Cockleshell Heroes' mission was a way of honouring these values.

Of course, the 'lark' I was planning along with five chums was a far cry from the realities of war, but knowing that I could in some way commemorate what many young men had actually *lived*, back in the dark days of the twentieth century, was a large factor in my initial enthusiastic response. My point is that taking part in a gentleman's expedition like this, to raise money for charity, was exactly the kind of *purpose* I could get behind – and having a sense of purpose is necessary in every endeavor, if you want to feel you've achieved any success! It was not just selfish 'fun', like my Paris to Athens hitchhike – we were raising money for charity. It was also something personally important to me. It's not enough to have any old purpose; you have to choose the right one, for the right reasons.

However, over the following weeks the gravity of Operation Cockleshell soon became apparent. We discovered that no other group had ever attempted to re-enact the entire raid from the sea, due to the unpredictable and ferocious tidal rushes at the mouth of the Gironde. What was more, the French authorities had stated that it was illegal to enter the Gironde by kayak as there had been so many fatalities over the years. We would be re-enacting the raid exactly 70 years after the original, from the very spot where submarine HMS Tuna had dropped the commandos off in December 1942, which was actually ten miles away from the entrance to the Gironde, and two miles offshore. In *kayaks*? Were we mad? There were so many things that could go wrong! I was close to feeling overwhelmed at so many different points. I don't think I would have been able to undertake this if I hadn't been well aware, thanks to the SAS, of the need for resources of *positiverosity*. Luckily my teammates also had this quality in spades – whatever they called it to themselves. Every time I felt overcome by what we had promised to do, I thought, *feel the fear and do it anyway*. I was motivated and I was resolved: over the years, I had proved to myself that positive visualisation is more powerful than we think.

We begged, borrowed and purchased the three two-man original-type Klepper Kayaks, and somehow convinced four other victims to join our crew. We needed to practise paddling on a regular basis – not easy for everyone, scattered as we were across the UK. Andy Hastings (a last-minute replacement team member) and Adam Rattray (the instigator) formed Team One, myself and Jimmy Wallace formed Team Two and Neil Laughton and Mark Beaumont, and in Team Three (Neil had been part of more than a few life-affirming experiences in my past). Mark Beaumont – now the famous cycling legend – had at that time recently returned from another water-related near death experience. Only two weeks prior to our kick-off in the Gironde, he was attempting to row the Atlantic from Morocco to the Caribbean. An accident in his team's boat meant they had to be rescued 28 days into their attempt to smash the 32-day record. Mark and five others were treading water in their boxer shorts for eighteen hours! It was a disheartening reminder that no matter the talent and hard work that goes into an expedition, sometimes fate has other plans. Well, failure happens in life – the only way to deal with it is to move on to the next challenge, as Mark – to his credit – did. Don't give in to the 'inner chatter' that tells you you've failed before you've even begun. Concentrate on the future; that was my idea! This is my philosophy with WildFox Events and in my life, and it has helped me a hundred times. What I call *positiverosity* is essentially keeping a tight grip on your thoughts, recognising and overcoming your nagging insecurities to ensure that you continue with self-belief to your goal. Think the impossible into possible, *make it happen*, adopt that 'can do' attitude.

Positiverosity and purpose dealt with, next up in the recipe for success in the Cockleshells venture was *planning*. When we commit to things we often underestimate the work and preparation that needs to go in: physical training, logistics, learning new skills, finding other aspiring adventurers to join our patrol, deciding on the right charity to support, reading endless books about 'Operation Suicide' (the title of which did not go down well with my wife) – not to forget planning a lecture tour for afterwards, in order to impart all the wisdom we'd surely learn. It would have been very easy to have accepted the invitation to join this commemorative raid, only to have then let Adam down by coming up with the usual list of excuses, which in most cases can simply be called 'lies'! In truth, we did a fraction of the training and preparation done by the original commandos. This was down to the fact that we were not living in barracks and were simply unable to train together. The original commandos trained day in, day out, and must have perfected their oarcraft before the operation. However, as I'd learned from various other missions, planning was necessary if we were going to get anything out of this incredibly risky adventure. Despite our separation, we managed to schedule a major training weekend in Portsmouth with all three teams, nicknaming it 'Operation Water Babies'. This was to be

our only opportunity to work together, test the equipment, work out what we were going to carry and also – the most important factor, some might say – test how the teams gelled together. In the event, the weekend was a great success. We bivvied on Hayling Island, and kayaked over twenty-five miles around the coast of Portsmouth past huge grey Naval gunships, and left feeling confident that we were ready for the real thing. Of course, our mission would pale into insignificance compared to what Hasler and his men achieved, we weren't going to be under threat from German snipers, nor were we going to undertake the trip in December, we'd go in August.

Soon August was upon us, and suddenly we were piled into my WildFox Discovery, heading to Bordeaux, pulling a trailer full of logistics. On the first night, we stayed with a friend who ran the Bordeaux Polo Club, sleeping in the clubhouse, which gave us enough space to sort out our incredible amount of kit into sensible sections. I even managed to give a polo demonstration to a few local club members. As I hadn't ridden for a few years, I could hardly walk afterwards – perhaps a lack of foresight and planning there. One thing positiverosity doesn't work well on is strained tendons...

And then D-Day arrived. The third golden principle is *practicality*. We headed for the embarkation port by the mouth of the Gironde. I was nauseous, and feeling an odd mixture of excitement and trepidation. We had read so much about these dreaded tidal rushes, but I for one certainly felt at that point that I still had no idea what we were getting into. *Had we done enough training; did we have enough action plans for the various things that could go wrong?* We had certainy prepared as much as we were able, but we were still at the mercy of chance. Well, we couldn't do any more now. Now was the moment to put into practice all our projections and dreams. What we'd imagined was soon to be a reality. As my friends, family and colleagues can tell you, I constantly go on and on about my belief that life must be filled with intensity and risk. Sometimes it takes these times, such as all those hours on the volcano crater in New Zealand, for us to truly appreciate that we are alive and what we have to lose, so we can reevaluate what really matters and see what difference we can make. My philosophy of philanthropy relies on the fact that I practice it in my own life. To motivate others, I have to show that I *do* what I believe – and this was one of the times where we were *doing*. 'Do the thing, and you shall have power.' It is simple, yet so easy to forget: practice what you preach.

After a good night's kip, we checked the weather, loaded up the support boat – skippered by a local French guy – and were off, hurtling along the French coast in the Bay of Biscay towards the setting sun. The Atlantic Ocean seemed smooth, and I remember almost like cream to my dazzled eyes. I looked at the stern expressions of my friends beside me, sunk in deep concentration and reflection, and knew that my own screwed-up face covered up the feeling of butterflies in my stomach, coming from thoughts of what the next six hours would entail – the first hours were the make-or-break of this six-day expedition.

We were going to the disembarkation grid where HMS Tuna had offloaded the intrepid teams

70 years earlier. We were relying on a local French-man who would drop us off in our 'Cockleshells' and then act as safety boat while we battled the tid-al rushes at midnight in pitch darkness. You would have thought that the terrifying witness accounts of the teams battling the tidal rushes in 1942 would have been enough to worry us, but life is a fun-ny thing. You can distract yourself so easily from fears of the future, but time marches on, and before you know it you're face-to-face with what you've dreaded – and yet, facing them in reality is com-pletely different, and far less terrifying, than you ever could have thought. This was a 'Feel the fear and do it anyway' moment.

The reality of the mission that had concerned us for the past couple of months, that we had fretted over, imagined, dreamed about and feared through-out the build up was now upon us. No more time for worrying. It was a relief that we could actually get on with it, just think about strapping ourselves in, finding the right rhythm, and moving on with it. In our modern lives, we don't often get the chance to put all our physical energies into a task, to throw ourselves in with pure force, until we're exhausted. Mental effort is often far more of a harmful stressor than physical, and I believe that shoehorning more physical, practical experiences into our lives can be good for us in many different ways. Practicality is such an important quality in the WildFox philosophy, both in terms of practicing what you preach, and in bettering yourself with a more practical lifestyle.

We dropped (metaphorical) anchor, sorted kit and disembarked from the French boat. Such a strange feeling to actually be underway! As we set off, I couldn't help constantly comparing the experience of my senses to that of the original teams, 70 years ago. The sound of water slapping against the side of the boat, the prickle of goosepimples on my skin in the sea air, the tang of salt in my nostrils were all the same physical sensations. Would they even have been noticing all that? They knew the Germans were aware of something going on. They had picked up HMS Tuna on their radar, and had sent a gunboat to investigate the area. We were dropped off in the evening, with the setting sun still glimmering on the horizon. The original team would have been dropped off in starlight. It is important to reiterate that obviously nothing we could do would replicate the actual atmosphere of the original escapade, apart from the journey itself. We did not have Germans hunting us down, August was undoubtedly warmer than December, and the weight carried by each man would have been considerably heavier – their limpet mines were not exactly light. However, our overarching disadvantage was that our bare minimum of training and preparation compared unfavourably to the weeks and weeks that the original team would have put in.

On the original raid one of the Kleppers caught on the conning tower of the sub (the part containing the periscope!) during disembarkation. Out of nowhere, the operative team was suddenly reduced by a quarter – as was the chance of success. Perturbing at this late stage, to say the least. At our own moment of disembarkation, I felt a sudden frisson of compassion for those forced to stay behind. I *felt* their frustration and the agony they must have felt to let their teammates down, not even able to launch!

We set off at a steady pace, paddling for an hour with a five minute break on the hour. Forget intensity and risk, this was the part where I had to exercise my hard-won skill of *patience*... I had not long to wait for adventure. Literally two minutes into the row, Adam lost his pilot light to the depths of Biscay Bay. We attached a back up Cyalume as a nightlight, and continued. We were now entirely immersed in reliving the adventure, referring back to parts of the (many) books we had read on the subject, trying to gauge what the original ten would have been feeling – what were the apprehensions of each man, knowing that his chance of survival was so small – shouting conversations from kayak to kayak. Our predecessors' knowledge of the tidal rushes were very poor (perhaps a reason for the absurd daring of this mission?) which ultimately resulted in the capsizing of one of their Kleppers at the outset of the voyage, in the rushes – and the death of two men from hypothermia. Perhaps a little more patience from their superiors would have helped those two brave men then – they might have waited yet longer for more detailed knowledge to come through from reconnaissance. However, it is always difficult to know when to seize the moment.

We, for example, had planned to enter the Gironde at midnight when the rushes were at their weakest. However, due to the usual pre-faffing with kit and assembly we had left one hour late. This small misjudgment of time played on our minds. We knew we would pay for it later on. Should we have postponed the launch, delayed for 24 hours? The weather conditions were perfect... we might not get an opportunity like this again ... we decided to crack on. Now was our moment, for better or worse. If you're too scared of starting, you'll never start. It wasn't exactly an auspicious beginning, but neither was it the worst possible time to start. Remembering that terrifying night on the New Zealand volcano, the one that still made my guts squirm whenever I thought about it, I knew that the point of *patience* is the end-point of *action*.

We imagined the German gun emplacements as they would have been, silhouetted along the sea coast, darker shapes against the dark sky. Hitler's indomitable Atlantic Wall – or so it seemed then: ominous shadows surrounding Europe. The original commandos did not know that a German gunboat was bearing down on their submarine launch site and they were also unaware of the horrors that were about to unfold for each one of them. Hasler, a distinguished, fair-haired young Dubliner, was just 28 at the time he planned and personally led Operation Frankton. He later recounted hearing a first terrifying roar as they paddled towards the estuary, before realising that it was the sound of rushing water. The group had little knowledge of tidal rushes, and before they had a chance even to call to each other, the tiny canoes were consumed by a huge surge of water, scattering them far and wide. Hasler could only watch as one of his boats capsized, and the two struggling commandos failed to get back in before it was lost to the waves. They swam to the shore, but were eventually captured and executed. Tidal rush No. 2 came next, and another boat went over. Again, due to the canoe's weighting, the men were unable to right it. Poor Hasler by this time must have been tearing his hair out. They had not even entered the Gironde and two boats had gone, with four men down plus the two that never made it off HMS Tuna. He must have been desperate with worry about what lay ahead.

We, however, knew all the bleak facts, and they constantly played on our minds. We did not know yet if we were going to experience similar conditions. Would there be three tidal rushes or just one? Had the tides changed much over 70 years? Had a sandbank shifted overnight? I was feeling almost sick with the adrenaline pumping through my veins. *Just take it easy, David. Just breathe. Patience, practicality, positive thoughts. Power through.* Were Adam and I being irresponsible, leading this team – men with wives and families – into such treacherous waters? Was it essential that we'd chosen to do it at night in the pitch black? What is it that makes us want to take unnecessary risks, why do we relish adventure and danger? Why does the recruitment increase rapidly when war is on? I was worried, but in my experience the risks I'd taken had turned out to be of great value later in life. Would my luck last? I wasn't invincible, however confident I was.

It was now dark and we were approaching four hours of steady paddling, having set off at 7.13pm (to be precise). We could just make out the shoreline and were happily in continual sight and contact with the other two boats. Adam's boat was in the middle as they possessed the weaker back-up light – unsatisfactory, really, but we were committed to just powering on. *No turning around now*, I thought. *No wimping out.* I was determined not to end this by kayaking for the shoreline. There was still so much ahead of us before we reached Bordeaux! Though we were well on our way now, I still felt rather as if I was about to make a parachute jump from a plane. Anticipation, fear, excitement and the actual feeling of blood pumping through my veins, beat by beat. I couldn't stop negative thoughts racing through my mind. *What will happen if a wave blows up and bowls us over? If the alert boat doesn't spot us in the dark? If our light isn't visible upside down? Could I manage to clamber back on board, or would the Klepper be submerged with the volume of water?* Thinking like this is not productive: no matter how much I worried, 'if'-ing and 'but'-ing, I just did not know. I would have to keep my head if I was going to complete this mission, I could not let myself panic. I had to be patient, just as I had been forced to be patient and distract myself as I sat through the blizzard in New Zealand, and managed to keep myself from going insane with fear... *I am going to stop worrying. I have learned the skill of patience*, I told myself. Oh, but *why* had the French authorities banned kayaks from going anywhere near the mouth of the Gironde, and how many deaths had been attributed to the deadly waters?

We were focusing on the shoreline and the other two boats in front and it was becoming apparent that our progress was slowing. The current was against us, indicating that our approach to the mouth of the Gironde was imminent. 'Come *on*, Jimmy,' I panted, 'Up the pace, man!' We redoubled our efforts, and yet we were still making slow progress against the waters. I snatched quick glances to the shore whenever possible, searching for reference points to measure our speed and progress, and then to the boats in front to reassure myself they were in sight and on course. We were at the back. If something happened, I did not fancy our chances of being rescued. We would be on our own.

It happened almost instantaneously: focusing on the dim lights of the two boats in front I noticed that they suddenly shot off to our left towards the North entrance of the Gironde. *Hey, what are they playing at?* Was my first, indignant, thought. They had changed course so dramatically, I wondered if they had taken a wrong turn. Before we had time to think, Jimmy and I were also being swept at an alarming pace out into the middle of the estuary's entrance. The power of the water was awesome; and we just had to go with it. Finally, it was happening.

'Manic pace, Jimmy!', I roared and we moved into an exhausting extra-fast mode of paddling. I had thought I couldn't be any more keyed up, but the fresh surge of adrenaline to my system was almost intoxicating. My heart was beating so fast it felt as though there was a humming in my chest as we frantically paddled, oars clashing as our timing fell out of sync and back in. All we could hear, apart from our own desperate gasps, was the massive roar of the rushes. We were in the midst of a witch's cauldron! This is what it was all about! It was the *pièce de la resistance* of this epic re-enactment. I have never felt more alive, more 'in the moment'. It was an incredible feeling, after having read so much about this, to live it. We too were fighting for our lives. It was magnificent. I was back to living what I now spent my time persuading others – in offices, conferences, auditoriums – to do. To challenge themselves and find that visceral thrill of experience that makes life worth living. When you experience intensity, risk and excitement, you are truly living. If I am evangelical about anything, it is about finding passion!

Then something extraordinary happened. The French skipper of the boat that had been escorting us simply took off through the rushes, heading for port, and vanished ahead. In our hour of greatest need and, indeed, possible death, the skipper just *buggered off*? Was he half-witted, or desperate to get back before the pubs closed? Extraordinary behaviour, and to this day we still have no idea why.

Anyway, we had better things to think about – like the fight for our own lives. If we'd fallen into this foaming whirlpool, we'd be pulled under instantly and not come up again – it was imperative for each boat to stay straight as it battled through the rushes, so as not to capsize. Kleppers are famously stable, but a moment's mishap could have us over in a jiffy. As with direct combat in war, everything could go to jack shit in seconds, despite all our planning, and leave each of us fighting alone for themselves. Jimmy and I could see the other boats criss-crossing in front of us, and then Adam and Andy's boat were behind us, the boat with no light. We were still paddling flat out, arms flailing. I was still looking to shore whenever I could, to gauge our progress by the lights and sea wall at the south entrance to the Gironde. We were making our way by literally inches, nearly deafened by the constant thundering of the waves and exhausted. We were also constantly shouting out to the other boats to check on their location and position. We could not afford to lose sight of the others. Neil and Mark were pushing on just ahead of us, but Adam and Andy were struggling behind. We could only communicate by hoarse yells. To look back would involve losing focus, and invited an immediate bowling-over. What happened if Andy and Adam capsized we thought? We would have to turn round and follow them. The rescue rib was now out of sight and we were on our own. I was pretty scared, I tell you, and for a moment considered roaring to Adam 'Make for the shore!' But I knew we had to persevere – it would have been dangerous, as well as lazy and defeatist to stop now. As with anything you choose to do, I had known I would feel fearful and unmotivated at points. I knew I would want to give up. However, as with my SAS selection, I blocked out that seductive voice in my head whispering 'Give up, you're tired!' Perseverance. There are better voices in your head to listen to.

Our pace was flagging, as there is a limit to how long a frantic paddle action can be sustained. We could now see a few people standing on shore, watching us. What were they thinking? *These nutters, what on earth are they doing kayaking at this time of night?* We made gradual progression, our hopes of success increasing as incrementally as we moved forwards, waves booming, regimental-sergeant-major bellows of communication – well, what an adventure this was turning out to be.

We were all coping with this extreme pressure in different ways, trying to just slog it out, persevere, trying not to think of the worst-case scenario of capsizing. It did not bear thinking about. The Kleppers did not have the usual flotation aids inside, and would fill up in an instant, giving us little ballast to hold on to. What were Moffat and Shard thinking of when they capsized in this exact location 70 years earlier, in freezing December waters? It must have been a desperate decision for Blondie Hasler to make. Having tried to tow them in, the darkness and chaos meant that he lost sight of them. There was nothing for him to do: he was forced to let them go. Their bodies were recovered on a beach some 60 miles north, several days later. They must have succumbed to the cold and simply run out of energy in freezing waters. How could you take on the Gironde tidal rushes swimming, let alone in a Klepper? Our mad mission was giving us the chance to have the maximum empathy possible with these men, as we went through so closely what they had gone through. This first phase of Operation Frankton cost Hasler two of his boats. Four men who would never return to Blighty. I thought once more of Wallace and his teammate who had capsized in the first tidal rushes and were able to make it to shore where they were captured by the Germans and shot the following day. As I paddled onwards thinking of these men in my exhausted state, it was their doggedness that motivated me to carry on. To be able to persevere, you must have something that makes you *want* to fulfill your task. My resolution to persevere was inspired by my purpose and the indefatigable perseverance of men before me.

I could only imagine what it must have been like for the original team, entering the Gironde so close to the harbour walls. I could picture them sweating and heaving their lungs out just like us; how on earth were they not spotted by the German searchlights, which were sweeping across the water as they entered the mouth of the Gironde? The Germans had been alerted by radar reports of the submarine HMS Tuna, so look-outs were anticipating something entering the estuary. However, they didn't anticipate the distinctive Kleppers, and the puny canoes slipped past without being spotted. Just as well they were hidden by the waves and the darkness, for how on earth would they have been able to defend themselves in any way from enemy fire, when both hands were required for the manic paddling?

Mark and Neil were now through the worst of the rushes and Jimmy and I were following behind, constantly bellowing out to Adam and Andy, but still not daring to look back. As we inched further into the river's great mouth, I felt my confidence growing. I now *knew* we could crack this! But we just had to keep pounding on steadily, without changing pace. I seemed to hear my grandfather's voice in my head, telling me *remember, my boy: patience*. Stick to it. To lose concentration now through a rush of optimism would be fatal to the mission. I needed to focus. These moments were still at the crucial point between success and failure, when continual steady effort would make all the difference, even though I was exhausted.

I remembered the feeling when I saw the final summit of the Ultra-Trail du Mont Blanc – the same feeling I had now: *I can do it. I can't do it. I must do it*. This summit was over slightly quicker than that mountain: ten minutes later, we had passed through the mouth and were cruising at slightly increased speed up the coast. We had made it through the biggest test of our mission! My heart was very full at that moment, as I rested my arms on the side of the canoe for a second. Unlike the members of Operation Frankton, the brave men who'd been in my mind every moment of this adventure, we had got through.

Exhausted and elated, we paddled towards our first *rendez-vous* of the expedition. We stumbled ashore, set up camp and tucked into our ration packs. Never had a steak-and-kidney ration-pack supper tasted so good! After devouring our meal, we chatted peacefully for some time by the fire, before we lapsed in companionable silence, reflecting on all that had happened. At this point after making it through the rushes, Blondie was aware he had now also lost a third team, Mackinnon and Conway, who were separated from the group as they entered the Gironde. Mackinnon and Conway never made it to Bordeaux, their boat snagged and sunk further up the Gironde. They then walked for a couple of days through France before being captured and shot by the Germans. It was sobering to think of their mission, and what depended on it. Our mission was to commemorate their bravery and to raise some funds for charity. The money we raised would go to the Royal Marines Charitable Trust Fund and The Stroke Association. Though only two of the Cockleshell Heroes had survived, perhaps we could still help some veterans of World War II. Of all the missions I have undertaken, this was perhaps the one for which I felt the strongest sense of purpose, personally and for a wider good.

We went on by following the same river route that Blondie would have taken, and stopping off at the various rendezvous points where he and his team would have laid up during daylight hours. The second night was spent by a shrimp platform which Neil and Mark managed to set alight with spilled methylated spirits. Thank God we were not on the real operation; this would have helpfully illuminated the entire team to the Germans. We paddled on, taking advantage of the tide when we could, and entered the ominous submarine pens of Bordeaux late on the third evening. Nothing much has been changed with these pens in the 70 years since wartime. Like imposing concrete garages lining the riverbanks, looming half- in, half-out of the water, the submarine pens echo with the eerie sound of water slapping on slimy concrete walls. Extraordinary architecture; and a privilege to be paddling around these relics of war. Still, I shivered as we passed through.

Arriving in Bordeaux by the river at midnight was an anticlimax after that brutalist reminder of great conflict. Twenty-first century nightlife in this student city was in full swing, with thudding music drifting from the open windows of bars and romantic couples mooning along the pavements. We, our minds still full of war and the Cockleshell Heroes, felt we were stepping into another time – if a few of those couples had looked up from their embraces, they'd have been taken aback to see a sweating, stinking group of men covered in the sludge of the Gironde clambering on to a jetty; dripping wet, ravenously hungry and searching for sustenance.

Of course, the *maître d'* of every bar, restaurant and café in Bordeaux turned up their noses at the sight (and smell) of us. We crashed out on the jetty, having consumed an ice cream, and waited for the tides to turn. At 2am we were off again! Back down the Gironde, following the river to Blaye. This small town was the spot where Blondie, his teammate and the last remaining boat paddled to, having secured eight limpet mines to a large German cargo ship and a small liner. The four men scuttled their crafts to avoid discovery and set out for the 100-mile walk north to Ruffec, where they planned to meet the Resistance. In order to increase their chances of survival the two two-man teams went separately on the back roads, each making their own way to Ruffec. Hasler and Sparks made it; Laver and Mills did not. Like Mackinnon, Conway, Wallace and Ewart, they were captured and shot by the Germans. So much for the Geneva Convention.

We followed the same route overland through the rolling Cognac country, taking fields and back roads, and visiting the various places that Blondie would have stayed at en route to Ruffec. The walk took us three days, sleeping under the stars. We were astounded by the total lack of human habitation along the route: where were all the people? Well, I wouldn't have blamed them if they'd all upped sticks and gone to the South of France – after all, it was August. I thought longingly of Nice beachfront in the 1980s. Here, rabid dogs and the odd ancient farmer were our only occasional company – and, worst of all, only one pâtisserie along the entire 100-mile walk! A cause for much complaint among our sweet-toothed team. Throughout our manic paddle, I had pushed through at least in part with thoughts of the plentiful, freshly-baked *pain au chocolat*, regular *chocolat chaud* and hot croissants I remembered from my Cote d'Azur hitchhike. Now, what did I say about finding a passion and a purpose?

The Cockleshell Heroes trip became the first of three commemorative expeditions. The following year I headed up a team to re-enact the journey of the Telemark Heroes when a group of brave commandos destroyed a heavy water plant in Norway which prevented Hitler from developing an atomic bomb. We camped in minus 26 degrees on the frozen lakes traversing the Hardanger Vida

following the original route of Operation Grouse. Our third and final adventure of the trilogy was commemorating the capture of General Kreipe in Crete by the two heroes Patrick Leigh Fermour and Billy Moss. An extraordinarily audacious endeavour where Patrick and Billy dressed up as Germans and ambushed the general's car and proceeded to drive unchallenged through 21 German roadblocks before walking Kreipe a hundred miles up and over Mont Ida, taking three weeks to reach the south coast safely, where they were met by commandos who whisked Kreipe off to Egypt. We followed Leigh Fermour's walking route over four nights, and met locals who remembered the mission first hand. Now, their audacity is controversial because of the loss of life that resulted as the Germans took out their anger and revenge on the villagers. I am a great believer in getting out there, and so there is always some new adventure forming in my imagi-

nation. I am always looking for ways to test myself
and improve my skills.

There are many other examples that I could
use to demonstrate the principles I want to share
with you, but they will have to wait for another
book. In 2006, I went to Morocco for a desert bike
ride on KTM450s, mastering the skill of ascending
a sand dune without losing control of the bike. On
another occasion I organised Operation Silver Bul-
let, another motorbike ride, but this time on Royal
Enfields with a mission to raise money for Mercy
Corps and a water project giving 600 families access
to clean drinking water in Darjeeling. The trip took
us one thousand miles. From the tea plantations of
Darjeeling eleven of us biked to Nepal, where we
did an 18-hour trek on foot before heading up to
Sikkim on the Enfields and then through the tiger
country of West Bengal and into Bhutan. Without conjuring up the adventure the sponsorship
wouldn't have been raised and those lives wouldn't
have been changed for the better. A key member of
our team was Lindsay Whitelaw, a founder of Artemis and a loyal supporter of WildFox Events.

One of my earliest international adventure challenges was the Hannibal Challenge. For
three consecutive years, I organised groups to
walk for two days in the footsteps of Hannibal
(without elephants). The route was from Guill-

estre in France through the Queras National Park and over the Alps via Pass de la Traversette, into Italy and the source of the Po River.

What joins all these adventures together is my ethos of making personal challenge life affirming, whilst helping others along the way. What better purpose than that of philanthropy!

POINTS FOR REFLECTION

- Those who spend their time worrying about what people think of them wouldn't worry if they knew how rarely other people think of them.

- You must know what you want.

- Do not wait for extraordinary circumstances to do good action. Try to use ordinary situations.

- Being able under all circumstances to practice five things constitutes perfect virtue. These five things are: generosity of the soul, sincerity, earnestness, kindness and gravity.

- Thought is the property of those only who can entertain it.

- Most of my life has been filled with the most terrible misfortune, most of which has not happened.

- The most evident token and apparent sign of true wisdom is a constant and unconstrained rejoicing.

CONCLUSION
A FINAL WORD ON THE SEVEN GOLDEN PRINCIPLES OF PURPOSE, PATIENCE, PRACTICALITY, PLANNING, POSITIVEROSITY, PERSEVER-ANCE AND PASSION

My aim in life is to *make a difference*. I've been passionate about motivating people for as long as I can remember and I'm fortunate that I've been helped by a wonderful power group of family, friends, colleagues, and supporters who get what I'm trying to do and rejoice in helping me do it. What I always come back to, time and time again, is that I've got a passion for encouraging people to achieve goals that far surpass their previous conscious aspirations. I've learnt the hard way through my adventures and experiences and it is fun (if sometimes a little humiliating) to share with others my mistakes. Failure can not be avoided if you want to Live Life Amplified, but should be embraced as part of personal growth. I hope to inspire those I meet to make more of their lives, and to make the most of being alive. Some of my schemes and adventures may have led me to sail too close to the wind at times, and it is by the grace of God that so far I've lived to tell the tale. Perhaps because of this I have learned some nuggets of truth the hard way. There is no doubt that one recognises all that one appreciates in life when staring death in the face. Imagine waking up tomorrow morning to discover you had lost all that you hold dear. How would that feel and how hard would you fight to regain your life today?

Through my business WildFox Events I have challenged thousands of individuals to dig deeper than they ever have before. I've appealed to them to go the extra mile, reap the rewards and sow seeds of change across the globe through charitable fund-raising. Over the years WildFox Events has evolved

and diversified. Change is good, it keeps one alert to new possibilities. I've recently been to China and the US looking for ways to promote my message of positiverosity and wherever I go I find people receptive to my ideas. WildFox Events not only organises big adventure challenges but also helps smaller groups in a variety of ways, be it through an initiative to give young school leavers practical skills in wood work, metal work and use of laser cut technology, or facilitating groups of teenagers leaving deprived areas of our cities to experience wilderness for the first time. I find myself saddened by the cotton-wool approach and risk averse attitude that is so prevalent today. It is killing off the spirit of adventure in young and old alike. Writing this book along with public speaking and mentoring are ways of reaching out to more people.

If you'd asked me as a teenager if I wanted to write a book nothing would have been furthest from my mind. I was an underachiever at school with undiagnosed dyslexia and yet I was highly competitive. I know the feeling of falling behind at a young age and not knowing what to do about it. Life can be so disheartening when you haven't found your purpose and you lack the confidence or ability to recognise it. Ironically, it is often the ones that love you most who want to protect you from falling, from failing, and yet to grow, you must be allowed to fail. Setbacks such as dyslexia can give one the advantage of having to think outside the box, to be positive and to be creative. My self-taught strategies, my own personal challenges and adventures and the training I had in the territorial army have equipped me to think on my feet in the face of adversity. Perhaps dyslexia has also enabled me to empathise with those in need of encouragement. It's using our own experiences to help us support those around us with kindness that counts.

Contemplate what the seven golden principles in this book mean for you. When I began this book I knew I was taking a risk, the risk of sounding patronising. Please be assured of my genuine desire to inspire change through my own reflections and if I succeed in doing so in some small way this was a risk worth taking. There is nothing ground-breaking within these covers, but sometimes all we need is a different perspective. If just one of my messages rings true for you then that is enough reward for me.

My aim is that this book will spark the potential in you to climb mountains or cross oceans, be they real or hypothetical. I hope these principles will give you the confidence to find a new more positive way to live your life, a more mindful way where you recognise that you are the master of the choices before you and have the ability to make a difference starting today. You may not share in my passion, but make sure you grasp yours with both hands and hold on tight. After all, life is about what you make of it. Never lose sight of what you truly want to achieve in your lifetime. Have Positiverosity!

ACKNOWLEDGEMENTS

I'd like to especially acknowledge the following friends who have also been inspirational in my life. You have read about Mark Beaumont, who continues to break the boundaries of long distance cycling. I'd also like to mention here my first cousin, William Fox-Pitt, World Champion rider and eventer – his total commitment to his passion and awesome focus of calm steely determination have made him a true hero; he demonstrates all the principles of this book.

Bear Grylls is a hugely influential positive role model for young people with his infectious enthusiasm – if anyone is *positiverosity*, he is! His career started out when my great friend Neil Laughton took him to the summit of Everest – the rest is history. Neil Laughton has so often been part of my adventures and his continuing work inspiring youth goes hand in hand with my philosophy of philanthropy. Another climbing friend is Polly Murray. From a young age Polly was a girl on a mission. She became the first Scottish woman to climb Everest and her determination has taken her on amazing adventures to The Arctic, The Antarctic, and The Amazon Rainforest. She stands out amid a sea of male explorers as a fantastic role model for girls the world over. Another cousin of mine who demonstrates how anything is possible with talent and determination is Birdy. Her meteoric career began when she won a music competition at the age of twelve and we are all very proud of her. Robin Seiger, a consummate professional on the public speaking circuit and bestselling author has offered advice each step of the way. Rob Wainwright, former Captain of the Scottish Rugby Team and for the British and Irish Lions, is a giant in world rugby who has a gift for encouraging determination in young people not to accept second place. Another famous Scots rugby international player and dear friend is John Frame. He has been a role model for me since we first worked together on the Caledonian Challenge, with his level headedness, his compassion, kindness and humility. Leven Brown, the record breaking ocean rower was in part motivated to start on his skippering career as a result of The Caledonian Challenge and has remained a good friend ever since. I must also mention Magnus Macfarlane Barrow, founder of Mary's Meals, who has proved that it's possible to turn an amazingly simple idea into an organisation feeding over 1.2 million children each day.

I am lucky enough to have many many loyal friends who have been part of the WildFox story. I'd have to write another book to mention them all but I'd especially like to thank Fi Lindsay, Tim and Sarah Willis, Grev Humphreys, Evelyn Walsh, Liz

Munns, Fiona Kirkwood, Eric and Leslie Pirie, Mike McCloy, Richard Kellett, Caz and Andy Hastings, Pete Waugh, John Morris, Andy Ferguson, Cameron Buchanan, Holly Hunt, Clarie Thompson, Magnus Frame, Tim Warren and Sue Currie. And of course I'd also like to thank all the hardworking team at Eyewear, especially Todd Swift, Alexandra Payne, Rosanna Hildyard and Edwin Smet.